# GOODBYE TRAFFIC TICKET

*A Fully Disclosed Remedy for All Traffic Fines*

GREGORY D. GARRETT JR.

ISBN: 978-1-5356-1304-0

# *Dedication*

I would like to dedicate this book to my $1^{st}$ teacher/mother Christine Henry for always believing in me and never doubting me for going after my dreams, vision, and goals knowing that I would stumble before I got it right and start seeing the fruits of my labor. $2^{nd}$ I'd like to dedicate this book to my sisters La Shonta C. Johnson who actually wanted to be a Lawyer, Felicia Garret-Turner (Fe-Fe made the best cakes), and Janet Garrett who was a Corrections Officer (may they all rest in power) whose unexpected death in 2012 on my mother's birthday sprung me into a chain of events that led me to what I believe to be the remedy of how to beat any and all traffic tickets and the pain that drove me to spend thousands of hours  researching this one particular subject. 3rd I want to give a special shout out to Taj Tarik Bey who's shoulders I stand on and is one of the reasons why I was able to write this book, and last but certainly not least my brother 'in law' Maurice Henry El Bey (aka Moorish Mo), a You-Tube sensation with well over 5 million views who is probably 20-0 in beating traffic tickets for providing me with 2 pieces of key information that I used in this book. I'm greatly appreciative of these 2 great warriors.

# *Disclaimer*

**I AM NOT A LAWYER** *nor do I advocate or promote myself as being a lawyer. I am only giving the readers general information based on my very own personal research and experiences and in no way, shape, or form am I giving anyone who read this book any legal or lawful advice. In fact do not consider this information legal or lawful advice. This book was written for informational, educational, and entertainment purposes only. Please be advised. If you want Legal or lawful advice I strongly urge you to go seek out a competent Attorney. Again this is not Legal Advice. If you are looking for legal advice I cannot personally help you in any way. If you in fact choose to use any of the information provided within this book please do so at your own risk.* **All information provided within this book is strictly my personal discovery** (*Writ in the Nature of Discovery) and nothing more. If you wish to confirm or deny any information found within these pages or don't believe in what's in this book in whole or in part then I strongly suggest that you do your very own research (and don't just believe) in various Law books i.e. American Juris Prudence, Corpus Juris Secundum, UCC Codes, Law Dictionaries like Valentines, Bouvier, Barron's Law, or Blacks Law, Supreme Court cases relevant in these matters, etc. that'll be listed all throughout this book as a source of reference to either confirm or deny these claims made by myself. Again if you choose to use any of the information provided within this book please do so at your own discretion. I am not to be held responsible in whole or in part any outcomes that one may experience if one chooses to use at their own free will rather you are successful in winning your case or losing your case. All efforts applied by you will fall on you and you will have no one to blame or praise except yourself. Please use caution and common sense if you decide to use any information within this book and do so at your own risk. Again please be advised.*

# *Opening Statement*

"We the people" is the 1st three words headlining the United States Constitution which was established in the late 1700's for the purpose of Europeans doing business in the land of America (America being a Continent) going back under the Articles of Confederation dating as far back to the 1100's with King John which was orchestrated by influencing Moors and Europeans which super seeds all State Constitutions which are all co-joined and is still valid today. We the people must learn the civics' of law within the Constitution, as it is the SUPREME LAW of North America being a REPUBLIC form of government for all of the States and not a democracy (see Article 4 Section 4 within the Constitution).

We the people must learn the and study the Constitution and know that we have inalienable and unalienable natural rights such as the right to liberty, life, freedom, learning, **TRAVEL OF THE LAND**, the pursuit of happiness, etc. The Constitution for the United States Republic of North America was established to protect the people's rights so that they would be in accord with the law pursuant to nature's law. However it is our responsibility to become familiar with law so that the unlawful procedures of traffic court and any other miscellaneous courts will no longer be a financial and mental burden upon us.

Remember all policies, penal codes, Statues, and ordinances etc. although having the appearance of law, is repugnant to the laws of the Constitution and is further null and void, meaning it is not withstanding and DOES NOT APPLY so long as you are not in agreement within the system. This appearance of law is called **COLOROF LAW**. This term "color of law" means distinguished from that which is real, therefore if it is not real then it doesn't exist and is further null and void to the law. All traffic courts are based and operate under color of law, and the indication of this is the yellow colored fringes which is against the law that carries a one year prison sentence (it's all about $$$$$) around that red, white, & blue business banner which is also a military flag that you see in the court room that is generally known to the public as the 'American Flag'. And by them having a military flag they're supposed to be in military uniform enforcing admiralty laws. We the people must again learn and know the supreme law of this land which is the Constitution, remember ignorance of the law is no excuse. Know and understand that the law is overwhelmingly on your side. I truly pray and meditate that all travelers and drivers who put their eyes on these pages develop a supreme understanding of this information and the confusion dissipated to the point of you all being able to see things from a more clear picture and perspective.

## *Thank You All*

I DEEPLY APPRECIATE ALL OF you who were willing to part ways with some of your hard earned energy/money and investigate by investing in this particular book to find out for yourself how traffic court and its overseers are robbing the people blind hook, line, and sinker allegedly. I chose to simplify every little detail right down to the last common denominator so that it would resonate with EVERYONE to invoke a thorough understanding of how this game within the courtroom is being played on us all in an unjust and unlawful manner allegedly. I promise you that this is unlike any book that you've read for I have spent over 4,000 hours researching this one particular subject along with much experience of training 100's with what I know and over 500 hours of court watching along with noting judge's responses to information within this book fine tuning and putting it to use inside the court room. I only ask that you keep an open mind as some or much of this information will be new to you. Be sure to investigate outside of this book to confirm or deny some or all of the information that are in between these pages that bests fits your needs. Be sure to visit the website at **www.goodbyetrafficticket.com**

# *Contents*

# *Chapter 0:*

## Citations Are Invalid Contracts

### WHAT IS A VALID CONTRACT?

According to the definition from the old ancient Indigenous people which pre dates every government known to man (Articles of Confederation, etc.) in the modern world in the Americas which goes back hundreds of thousands of years and beyond is explained as the following. A Contract *means to draw; to agree upon; to establish by agreement; to enter upon; and to undertake, mutually.*

Contracts are essentially ***manifest written or oral agreements*** or covenants that are mutually entered into by **two or more parties**; involving or bringing the said parties into conditional obligations which are enforceable by Law. Contracts may be classified in accord with the nature and elements that initiated their constructions, etc. A Contract is thusly a '*Promissory Note*' or '*Covenant*' made between the *identified* and *competent parties (2 or more people)*that '*Creates*' '*Modifies*' or '*Destroys*' a *legal* relation, upon sufficient and non-vague *considerations*, which demands of *a party to the contract* to do or perform, *or not to do or perform*, a particular thing.

A Contract must show, in its preliminary making and construction, the clear and '*Substantive Offer*' made by one party, and demonstrates the '*Mutual Acceptance*' affirmed by the other party.

A Contract must *be producible* (and exist in evidence) upon demand made by either party to the Contract, which, in itself, may be in question, dispute, or controversy.

A Contract must be produced in manifest writing, (*evidence*) and *contain the details* of the agreements, debts, or promises, with all the terms, the obligations, and the conditions, which clearly show and serve as proof that a valid and enforceable obligation, promise, or debt, exists.

A Contract must be a deliberate and *conscious agreement* made between *competent* parties.

A 'party' to a contract cannot be a *minor*.

A Contract must be entered into by **'free-will'**.

**A Contract must not be created under *threat, duress,* or *coercion (a police officer will arrest you if you don't sign the ticket)*, lest it be void in law.**

A Contract must be *substantive* and germane to the *subject matter*.

A Contract must be of *legal* consideration. It cannot be based on an unlawful consideration.

A Contract must possess *'Mutuality of Agreement'*, and *'Mutuality of Obligation'*.

A Contract must not be *vague, unclear, uncertain*, nor can it contain terms or conditions that *are not ascertainable*.

A Contract must show *valid signatures of the parties* to the Contract instrument, in order to verify its validity in law. **If a Contract *fails to satisfy* the *laws that govern its making or construction*, then any such *Contract* is void *Ab Initio*, and is considered "*dead in the view of the Law*".**

Also a 'Contract' founded on a base consideration, or against good morals is null and void. Base in law it means that which is low, inferior, foul, servile, of a subordinate degree or nature; impure and adulterated or alloyed. Null is a term in Law which means, "Naught" and being of no validity or effect in law. Null is usually conjoined with the word "void": as 'Null and Void'. In the law that governs 'Contracts' or 'Statutes',

Null and Void is used, applied, ruled, or recognized to establish, declare, or proclaim that such a low, inferior, foul, servile, or base Claim, Claimant, Judgment, Summons, Ticket, Bill of Exchange, or that any other Contractual Instrument, (befitting to the nature of the foresaid descriptions) are dead in law, colored, fraud, non-binding, unclean, and having no legal force or effect. Now that you have a thorough understanding of contracts imagine going into a fast food restaurant and your standing in line waiting to order some food and you thought about another place that has your favorite tacos and you instantly had a change of heart and decided to go their instead. So as you're about to walk out the Manager leaps over the counter, jumps in front of you, and told you that you MUST purchase food from their food place and if you didn't you would be arrested for not AGREEING to eat there. Well just by me explaining that scenario to you anyone with common sense would think that it wouldn't happen to them because that would be absolutely ridiculous however when an Officer pulls you over and demand that you sign the traffic ticket or do BUSINESS and contract with them (don't they pass out business cards) which is a adhesion type of contract and comply with them but yet you didn't verbally agree to the contract at the restaurant. Any judge or lawyer highly educated knows that all contracts are optional and that you never have to enter into a contract if you don't want to. The only difference is that one contract is written while the other is verbal but nonetheless their both are still binding contracts in a court of law. This is absolute law so if any Officers or anyone for that matter who may be reading this book who may disagree with some or all of this piece of information just try and grasp the possibility (provable facts) that you may have been inadequately trained for the purpose of profit through extortion and racketeering methods with a great deal of implemented deception. And by default this make you guys "Highwaymen". Highwaymen are persons who would literally rob travelers on the highway. I sometimes refer to cops as "revenue raisers" sent out to rob people of their money and property to pay for judges' salary, and the debts the state owes to the international bankers allegedly. These types of thieves used to travel and robbed by horse as mounted highwaymen. What I mean by this is if someone owns a car outright and it's not "registered" and a police officer comes along and pulls someone over based on the way penal codes are set up that will allow an officer to "take" that car off the road (thievery of property and liberties) hence Highwaymen. This is not me trying to put police officers down or make them look bad because in all honesty is not their fault per say their just performing their duties with a very limited amount of information and knowledge kept away from them for obvious financial reasons. I personally think that many officers do a great job (this only applies to the few who uphold the Constitution and truly understand it) keeping communities safe with a very low crime rate in cities given the proper man power. It's just that they didn't explain to you guys and allow you to truly study it in great detail (like they did with Penal Codes) about the 2 Constitutions that all of you took an Oath on (which makes all of you liable) to uphold, preserve, and defend against all enemies foreign and domestic (domestic meaning the people who may be standing right beside you that might be in violation). They added some things called Penal Codes and Ordinances to curb the real Law that's within the Constitution. The Constitution actually supersedes all penal codes and statues. I mean think about it if these codes were so important or are actually considered law why didn't they have you all take an Oath on it? I'll tell you why because it's not law. No matter how many of you may be interpreting this information you can't get around established facts and you surely can't get around the Law. They gave you bits and pieces of Title 18 of the United States Codes but only so that you would think or 'believe' that you had exactly what you needed to implement and enforce the Law as a whole while on duty. That couldn't be further from the truth. Have you (any officers) ever looked up any case laws and saw with your own eyes what higher courts have ruled on based strictly on the law when it pertains to traffic matters? And just so you know anytime a court higher than traffic court like a State Supreme Court has ruled on a case and no appeals or disputes came after the ruling especially when they deal with law coming directly from the Constitution that case can be used later as a reference or as a reinforcement to another case at a later date as evidence. One of the keys issues is that they've never inform the people that Traffic Court was never established, written, and or ordained within the Constitutional fold of Government? In fact the Highway Patrol used to be called "the Enforcement Division for the Department of Motor Vehicle" (DMV) which is just an extension of the DMV. This means that there job is to enforce codes and safety on commercial vehicles only and people who get paid to drive like truck drivers, uber, taxi, & pizza delivery drivers. They could've easily called traffic court DMV court. I think/believe that they called it traffic court to have people believe that it is legit especially now since tickets are listed as criminal offenses even though traffic offenses are crimes not punishable by imprisonment which means it's not a real crime. Think about that because we have a very serious issue. On one hand we have police agencies all across America and other parts of the world that unlawfully enforce citations or contracts onto the people and on the other hand we the people from all walks of life being unlawfully given citations and processed through these fraudulent courts and have been extorting trillions of dollars if not more since its inception. It even states it in the California Constitution that you guys took an Oath on isn't supposed to be writing these tickets. It's called a Bill of Attainder before they changed the name of what they call it (only to throw you off) to what's now being called citations, fines, and traffic tickets. These tickets are known as adhesion contracts which are unlawful under Contract Law and within the Constitution. It goes even further and says that anything (written material) posing as Law especially in contradiction after the Constitution shall not be law and further is null and void to the law however you guys are pushing these Penal Codes ignorant to these facts (as a substitute) when it's in direct conflict with real law, the Constitution. Another part of the deception is being properly identified. Think back and try to remember the last time you (Officers) approached a car and provided 3 forms of identification for the person you stopped as official proof that you are in fact who you say you are. If you didn't know that it is by law that you provide those 3 items when asked by any person(s) during these traffic stops (a form of an arrest without a warrant) and to not show them as proof you my friend are violating the Law which is a felony and criminal in nature. It's under something that is called "General Police Order" which is on the books. These 3 items are their bond number or badge number along with a proper dress code or in police uniform, their Oath of Office and something that is called Delegation of Authority Order (DOAO). Today they only require a badge number, uniform, and business cards. This bond is indemnity insurance and all corporations must have indemnity insurance in order to operate in business. When a government agency claims that they have a "blanket bond" (one bond that covers many Officers) and not individual bonds on each public servant, they are letting us know that they are operating as a for profit foreign European private corporation and in addition they are not government. Within the Constitution it states that all public servants must be bonded. They are the only ones who can act, engage in an action of any kind therefore their actions and public performance has to be bonded to ensure that they will always protect the people. This is truly their only function. After knowing this when approached by an officer and he or she hands you a business card are not properly identifying who you are in law because it works both ways. If someone showed you a business card and said hears my identification you wouldn't be satisfied right. So if we want to be fair then you have to admit that a business card is not sufficient enough. In fact the last time we even had official police officers with these credentials on record was last documented way back in 1929 that actually had these items on their person. In addition a real and legitimate officer is ELECTED by the people of the State that there in whom the people feel they can trust. Question.....is cops hired or elected? Regardless if an Oath was taken. When police officers are hired and not elected they are committing fraud unknowingly and unaware. And anyone who receives compensation automatically gets demoted from an official Police Officer to a mere private Security Guard. And as an armed guard you're supposed to have a gun permit. I was taken aback when I found out that police officers are actually employees for the corporation of the U.S.A. Incorporated and were purposely put into place as private contractors for unjust imposed contracts. So what I am saying is that the United States is a business and not a place or territory that most of us think or believe it is. As you read more and more throughout this book the evidence will show and prove that if you are out here posing as law enforcement and writing tickets you are in fact and in law violators of the Constitution rather you like or not, or believe it or not. I wonder how many officers are going to stop writing tickets and uphold their obligations on their sworn in Oath after reading this? I'm so curious. I'm thinking if I should write a part 2 to this book explaining in detail exactly how to sue cops/judges (some fired) that is in violation of the law. I don't see cops or judges letting up on us as far as this extortion process go. We simply have 2 options here, we're either going to change the way we operate within the Constitution by getting a better understanding of it and honor it or someone(s) is going to have to pay for all these injuries that this system is causing. Since police officers took the Oath that makes them liable under the law. This situation is no different than when a child acts out and gets out of line and the parent gives them an ultimatum of either correcting the error or punishment as a means of discipline. Me personally I get the fact that it's bigger than these foot soldiers (officers) doing what their being to do and following orders. This thing goes back to the beginning of the United States Company being incorporated in Puerto Rico and Washington D.C. being a sovereign state controlled and owned by the Royal Crown of England and Vatican City. And everything that's being done in traffic court is being done under Roman Civil Law. Roman Civil Law is a subset of Cannon Law. Cannon Law comes from the Vatican and the Vatican I believe is run by evil men. I'm not even going to go into details about the banks that control our debt money system. You may be thinking to yourself how does this guy know for sure that the United States is in fact a Corporation and not the actual territory that they portray it to be? It's under Title 28 USC 3002 Section 15 (A) (B) of the Uniform Commercial Code (UCC) and it states that the **UNITED STATES** is a **FEDERAL CORPORATION**. It's also listed within the business of **Dun & Bradstreet** as THE UNITED STATES. These territories obviously have its fair share of law and money problems that are in fact deliberate.

### *Title 18, Part I, Chapter 13 §241 of United States Codes*

*If two or more persons conspire to injure, oppress, threaten, or intimidate any person in any State, Territory, Commonwealth, Possession, or District in the free exercise or enjoyment of any right or privilege secured to him by the Constitution or laws of the United States, or because of his having so exercised the same;* ***or*** *If two or more persons go in disguise on the highway, or on the premises of another, with intent to prevent or hinder his free exercise or enjoyment of any right or privilege so secured—They shall be fined under this title or imprisoned not more than ten years, or both; and if death results from the acts committed in violation of this section or if such acts include kidnapping or an attempt to kidnap, aggravated sexual abuse or an attempt to commit aggravated sexual abuse, or an attempt to kill, they shall be fined under this title or imprisoned for any term of years of for life, or both, or may be sentenced to death.*

### *Title 18, Part I, Chapter 13 §242 of United States Code*

*Whoever, under color of any law, statute, ordinance, regulation, or custom, willfully subjects any person in any State, Territory, Commonwealth,*

*Possession, or District to the deprivation of any rights, privileges, or immunities secured or protected by the Constitution or laws of the United States, or to different punishments, pains, or penalties, on account of such person being an alien, or by reason of his color, or race, then are prescribed for the punishment of citizens, shall be fined under this title or imprisoned not more than one year, or both; and if bodily injury results from the acts committed in violation of this section or if such acts include the use, attempted use, or threatened use of a dangerous weapon, explosives, or fire, shall be fined under this title or imprisoned not more than ten years or for life, or both, or may be sentenced to death.*

# *Chapter 1:*

## So You Got a Traffic Ticket

*I always tell people that when those red, white, and blue lights come on and you are being pulled over by an Officer (this severely violates their Oath for non-emergencies) to always be respectful even if they are not courteous to you for your and their safety (mainly for your safety). In the act of being pulled over before coming to a complete stop you should be rolling all of your windows up with the exception of the driver window which should be about 6-8 inches below from the top which is a safe space opening for you and the officer. You should also lock all doors before you are pulled over and if asked to step out you should lock all doors behind you. During the traffic stop you should always keep your hands visible on the steering wheel and be sure to make all movements slowly letting the officer know exactly where you're going to reach while you are reaching for items in your car. In fact you shouldn't be reaching for anything (or unnecessary movement in general) but paperwork if you choose to. In their defense they don't know who you are just the same that you don't know who they are. If by any*

*chance that you are in a place with little to no lighting especially if no one is around you might want to let the officer know that you do not feel safe in that particular street/road that you are on and if it's okay to go to the next gas station or whatever's nearby. In most cases they usually don't have an issue with it as long as you're respectful about.*

*The reason why I bring this up is just in case their squad car or body cam isn't recording by being directly behind you with the dash camera recording your car or you just being in a vulnerable position especially without any witnesses. When or if asked by the officer "do you know why I pulled you over"? Never ever tell on yourself (don't admit or deny anything with police) by admitting to some act or anything which would cause you to probably receive more fines on your citation or even possibly going to jail (at any time you can choose to remain silent and not answer their questions) not to mention the* 5th Amendment *of the Constitution which states that* no person shall be compelled in any criminal case to be a witness against him or herself, nor be deprived of life, liberty, or property, without due process of Law. *This would apply in court and or if a person was under arrest. The reason the 5th amendment is mentioned because when a cop pulls you over you are at that very moment under arrest because you cannot physically leave their presence until they are done dealing with you. To be detained is a form of an arrest. Now the 4th Amendment states that* ***"the right of the people to be secure in their persons, houses, papers, and effects, against unreasonable searches and seizures, shall not be violated".*** *An unreasonable search would be to search a car without the permission of the owner, or to use trickery so as to confuse someone into allowing an Officer to search one's property. So what this means is that when you get pulled over and an officer ask to see your personal property also what they know to be your identification or 'driver's license', insurance papers, and registration, or anything else for that matter they truly don't have the right to do so. When it comes to actually showing your I.D. to a police officer for the sole purpose of verifying who you are this is truly not required by you or any other individual just so that they can run a back ground check to be nosy. It is illegal for them* *to force you to produce I.D. especially when no crime has been committed by you or you're not being identified as a possible suspect in their quote unquote investigation of a crime that recently occurred. One particular Supreme Court Case ruled that a police officer CANNOT ARREST a citizen merely for refusing to present identification* ***Kolenderv. Lawson*** *(461 U.S. 352, 1983). Just because you don't want to show I.D. doesn't mean a crime is being committed based on what a crime is rather injury or damaged property. This may sound a bit farfetched for some to believe but we can sue police officers (file a complaint but take it a step further and sue them) for an illegal arrest and resist arrest with impunity. Here are some case laws that are in support with what I'm telling you guys. "An illegal arrest is an assault and battery". The person so attempted to be restrained of his/her liberties has the same right to use force in defending him or herself as they would in repelling any other assault and battery". (****State v. Robinson****, 145 ME. 77, 72 ATL. 260). "Each person has the right to resist an unlawful arrest. In such case, the person attempting the arrest stands in the position of a wrongdoer and may be resisted by the use of force, as in self-defense". (****State v. Mobley****, 240 N.C. 476, 83 S.E. 2nd 100). "One may come to the aid of another who is being unlawfully arrested, just as he/she may where one is being assaulted, molested, raped or kidnapped. Thus it is not an offense to liberate one from the unlawful custody of an officer, even though that person that's being arrested has submitted to such custody, without resistance". (****Adam v. State****, 121 Ga. 16, 48 S.E. 910). "These principles apply as well to an officer attempting to make an arrest, which abuses their authority and transcends the bounds thereof by the use of unnecessary force and violence, as they do to a private individual who unlawfully uses force and violence". (****Jones v. State****, 26 Tex App.I;* ***Beaverts v. State****, 4 Tex. App 1 75;* ***Skidmore v. State****, 4 Tex. 93, 903.So when it comes to proving proof of who you are to law enforcement make sure that you use your discretion. As far as you giving them your social security number for the love of God don't. This is truly one item that they definitely do not have legal access to unless they have it in writing from all necessary parties with signatures. Just read the back of your social security* *card and see what it says. There are a few bad apples who will take your private information and use it for illegal activity. Understand that they're criminals in every facet of life. Even if you didn't want to use your social security number in the public you also have that right. There's something called a CPN along with trade line(s) and that is short for credit privacy number that can be used for the same purpose as your social security number. A person can gain access to great instant credit business or personal if one were to ever apply for one. Just be sure to investigate before you invest in one. Question......is insurance optional or mandatory? When was the last time you were forced to get fire insurance, life insurance, earthquake insurance, gap insurance for your car, cell phone insurance, or flood insurance? Never right? So for them to say that you "must have car insurance" is essentially slavery. Anytime anyone/system force you to do something against your will is essentially slavery. Now I'm not saying to not show them proof of your car insurance or proof of registration however in law it states that you don't have to. I suggest that if they become aggressive towards you if you choose to not show them your personal property to show them anyway under duress to avoid bodily harm or worse death. However in today's modern time giving the fact that we live in a police state and many of the laws have been twisted and distorted to the point that most people don't really know what's really what. What all of us travelers have to realize is that all sworn in Officers that go through vigorous training through the academy are in my opinion inadequately trained. You see when they are being taught various things whether it be paperwork, tactics training, PENAL CODES, etc. towards the end right before they graduate they have them sign and agree on both Constitutions which are contracts. And this is where the lie kicks in. Although they have agreed to uphold, preserve, and defend the Constitution against all enemies or violators foreign and DOMESTIC they never fully explain to them exactly what's in the Constitution that applies to their profession and how to administer the Law and truly defend it which in turn by the way is in direct conflict with the penal codes, Statutes, and Ordinances which is why they don't go over it with them vigorously like they do with those penal codes. They (cops) are literally being played on this piece of information. If they don't have the proper information they cannot perform their duties properly just the same if someone neglect to give their body's proper nutrition with high amounts of minerals their bodies would start to break down over time and become sick. Letting the police know that you are aware of your rights makes them aware about violating your rights. Each State has its own Constitution however it states in the California Constitution (Ratified in 1849) under Article 1 section 16 that No* ***bill of attainder (citations),****ex post facto law(anything written posing as law in contrary AFTER laws were originally written), or law impairing the obligation of contracts, shall ever be passed. A bill of attainder (also known as an act of attainder or writ of attainder or bills of pains and penalties) is an act of legislature declaring that a person or group of persons are guilty of some crime and punishing them, often without a trial which is unlawful and not a part of the proper legal process which is essentially why it is declared to be banned in the California Constitution. Which basically means that an Officer cannot initiate a complaint because it's not a real crime (no injury was caused, no property damage, or nothing was stolen from the officer or anyone else) in other words it is fake or better yet a fraud. A natural person or victim would be the one that would complain against you in the matter of a real crime if it ever took place. So after receiving that citation and after reading this book know that you can go in to court and win your case and not give a dime. Traffic tickets are actually lawsuits which mean that they are suing you for breach of contract even though the DMV contract for travelers is Void Ab Initio. And please if you ever in the future get a traffic ticket don't argue with them. The people out there that argue only argue because they don't know……Anderson Silva is not going to argue with someone and make a scene but if anyone were to step to him they would get a brutal beating from that man. I don't say this to be a butt however most officers in my opinion are just programmed idiots that just do what they are told to do and don't question or challenge any of those policies that are in* ***direct conflict*** *with the Constitution that they are enforcing. And it's not being challenged because they simply aren't keenly* *aware of key information that's laid within the Constitution. During a traffic stop  if you ever get a citation let's say 70 miles or more away from where you live always ask for something that's called a* **"CHANGE OF VENUE" or a "county seat"**. *And if they don't know what that is ask them to get their sergeant out there on the scene to be sure that you receive this benefit. Since the officer is claiming that you committed a crime that means that the burden is on them to come to you in your city or town (jurisdiction) and get your case heard in a court room near you. So if you live in Los Angeles California and a cop gave you a ticket in Las Vegas Nevada that Officer would have to come all the way to Los Angeles to prove their case and if they don't show up they automatically dismiss your case. Another thing to watch out for during a routine stop is when they ask you if the address on your license is current. Beware if it differs from the one on your license that will be another charge that would be added to your ticket so don't give them any added information if it differs on your license because you have the right to remain silent. And when you give your autograph (signature) on your Citation may I suggest that you sign starting with your name followed by UCC 1-207, UCC 1-308, "under duress",  "without prejudice" or "under protest" and be sure to circle your signature because criminals do tamper with evidence. If at all possible get your license renewed and sign it with the UCC codes so that it pops up on your picture I.D. If the police don't have probable cause (a lawful reason) to search your car like a strong smell of weed, (even this has been deemed as insufficient evidence due to lack of proof) visible gun (Right to bear Arms), being intoxicated, please do not allow them to search it. What if the car you are in rather if it's yours or not had some drugs, needles, or something illegal in it that you knew nothing about especially if you have people that are constantly in your car. Have you given it a thorough inspection to make sure there's nothing in it that could possibly get you thrown in jail? This is one of the few reasons why you should never allow them to search your car. If you've paid attention as to* ***HOW THEY ASK YOU TO SEARCH YOUR CAR*** *notice that their very clever in their approach. They'll say something like "oh you don't mind if we search your car do you"?*

*Or "you're not carrying any guns or drugs in your car are you"? So you wouldn't mind if we search it because you don't have anything to hide. And most people say "oh no I don't have anything to hide go right ahead" and allow some of these disrespectful Officers to ransack through your belongings breaking some of your property in the process which by the way is a violation of their Code of Conduct. When this clever use of language is used against you just politely say* "I understand that you guys have a job to do officer and I get that however I don't consent to any searches" *(at least not without a warrant). And what the Police are not telling people from what I believe is because they truly don't want you to know is that* **THEY HAVE TO GET PERMISSION FROM YOU**. *This means that you at that time have the power. Remember that the law is on your side in the matters of Officers searching your vehicl**e.*** When this is done just be prepared and state the *line above and stand firm in your answer. Another part of the game that they're not disclosing to the public is that car insurance companies buy radar guns for police stations free of charge to ensure both parties make more revenue. When Officers catch more people speeding and the person is found guilty and the point goes on their record their insurance rates goes up and thus charged more money for the same insurance that's allegedly optional. So not only are you being charged for the citation and time out of your day spent in court it's on going because you now have to pay through the nose because of your spike in insurance rates going up to about 20-25% over the next 3 years. In many cases a "driver" may not have a moving violation point however it's still a vicious unlawful cycle that there put through having those added charges and all.*

### *MIRANDA WARNING*

***1. You have the right to remain silent.***

***2. Anything you say can & will be used against you in a court of law.***

*3. You have the right to an Attorney being present while being questioned by law enforcements.*
*4. If you cannot afford an Attorney one will be appointed to you for your protection of rights.*
*5. You can at any time decide not to answer any questions by authorities or make any statements.*

*WAIVER*

*Do you understand each of these rights that I have been explained to you?*

*With these rights in mind do you still wish to talk to us now? A famous case known as "Miranda v. Arizona" in the 1960's brought this issue to the forefront of our Justice system and made it mandatory for law enforcement to make aware of the rights of the citizens if they are to be held under arrest and taken into custody.*

# *Chapter 2:*

## Origin of Drivers and Travelers

The origin of "driving" for the United States became legalized around 1915 when the Legislature gave the task to the State Treasurer. This entire process was originally and specifically designed for "drivers" only based on its definition. Before that the Secretary of State normally took care of vehicle registration from 1901 to about 1913. If you owned a traveler conveyance (car) back then the registration fees would have cost you about $2 or so. The registration sticker was only given to those who had proper front and back lighting, good brakes, and a horn or a bell. The first Department of Motor Vehicle (DMV) was implemented in 1915 with the enactment of Senator E.S. Birdsall's "Vehicle Act of 1915". On file that same year they initially had about 191,000 people to register their cars. There were a few other companies that set out to do the same thing as the DMV however by 1931 the DMV became the standard and "go to place" to get ones car registered. Licenses were required around the same time as fees for registration of one's car. Now the concept of insurance is as old as one can imagine. If you go back just a few hundred years they had insurance on slaves, ships, boats, crops of all sorts within various parts of lands, and even life insurance. Here in the U.S. they gave the credit of the genesis of the insurance industry to Benjamin Franklin for initiating a company that offered fire insurance. Car insurance was truly only introduced because of the overwhelming number of car accidents that were accumulating all over the United States due to no traffic lights to alleviate and or prevent these things from happening. When this happened many companies saw a huge opportunity to make an extreme amount of money. I mean when you think about it and giving the fact that no one is perfect more cars over the road would naturally equal more accidents over the road. This also led to arguments over who was in the right and who is to be held responsible for injuries and damage to property that was a direct effect of these car accidents. This growing issue of traffic accidents was greatly reduced thanks to a man by the name of Garrett Morgan. He was the one that initially invented the traffic light. In the early 20's he was a local business man that sold various types of clothing out of Cleveland Ohio and produced many other inventions as well. What prompted Morgan to even invent the traffic signal was an accident that he witness first hand in his community that led to the death of a little girl and a horse between a horse and carriage and a car. Before these particular invention police officers from all over would hold up signs and blew whistles on the streets informing people when to stop and when to go. This method was almost useless because many officers were getting side swiped and some were even getting killed in the process because many people weren't able to see the signs in some aspects because of blind spots on the road. In today's modern time on average roughly about 40,000 people die in the United States every year due to car accidents for various reasons. I've noticed in other countries where the driver training courses are more detailed, more hands on, and more time spent in learning have less than half the mortality rate than the U.S. with a much bigger population. In essences he has helped to save many lives with his invention. Garrett was also the 1st Moor to own a car in his city. In 1923 he was officially issued a patent for the very first traffic signal. It actually wasn't the colored lights that we see today. It was just words on signs held high that told people when to stop and when to go. General Electric Company was the one who actually changed it to color lights from copying the railroad service. They paid Morgan a whopping $40,000.00 for the rights to his patent thinking that it would in turn make a huge profit and they did. In today's time that $40,000.00 would equate to almost a million dollars. It eventually went worldwide for General Electric and paid huge dividends for the company. The first traffic sign in the United States was set setup in Cleveland Ohio on east 9th street and Euclid. When these traffic lights started to spread, newspapers were suggesting to "drivers" (travelers by definition) to remind themselves of the colors of red, green, and yellow and which meant which by putting a note and gluing it in their hats as a reminder. In Garrett's later years in the 30's he ran for city council because he felt many injustices for his people within the city in which he lived. Although he didn't get a seat on the board he remained a positive influence in his community. He became legally blind as he grew older due to glaucoma. Glaucoma is something that can now reversed and or eliminated by herbs like Moringa **(gochefahki.com-Dr.Sebi.com-aboriginalmedicalassociation.com)** and a alkaline diet that offsets diseases in the body. Morgan passed away August 27th 1963 at the age of 86. In terms of insurance one of the first and biggest names for car insurance was called Travelers (right to travel) Insurance Company. It was originally design to insure horses and carriages. Their very first policy for a car being insured was for a man named Gilbert L. Loomis back in 1897 although on paper it was Dr. Truman Martin of Buffalo, New York in February of 1898. It was the state of Connecticut that made it "law" or mandatory to except financial responsibility to other drivers back in 1925. There was 2 ways of proving that one was insured. One way was to show proof of insurance and the 2nd way was to show proof of financial stability. And as each state adopted these ways and methods the right to travel aspects were overlooked and slowly faded out as more and more people viewed what they were doing as driving and not traveling. In our more current times we as a whole are partly in some aspects oblivious to these terms especially from a law perspective. Now let's go into these two terms that many people are for the most part unaware of in terms of the way we view them. When people hear that term "driver" they automatically think/assume without putting any real thought behind it what the term driver really means. People in general believe what the "tell a lie vision" or T.V. tells them not to mention all of these commercials and court shows that use the word driver over and over when pertaining to a person behind a wheel in their vehicle and it gets ingrained in peoples' minds and they eventually through constant repetition just accept what they see and hear on T.V as truth when in fact they have no clear and precise understanding of what that word means exactly. Not all but many people never even looked up the word driver based on its lawful definition. There's another word that people are also familiar with but do not associate this word too often of being behind the wheel and that word is called traveling. A traveler is one who travels in any way. This includes every person that's on the road who uses their personal vehicle for personal reasons. In other words when you are traveling in your car weather you're going to work, school, church, running errands, etc. you are in fact not driving but traveling. This also includes how you are actually getting around as your method of travel. So this would include the use of a skate board, scooter, a bike, snow boards, cars, roller skates, jogging using your own two legs, hover board, etc. As long as you're in motion creating space from your starting point you are traveling. Now on the other hand when a person is driving they are one employed conducting business i.e. making money. This means that cab drivers, Fed Ex drivers, truck drivers, pizza delivery drivers, limo drivers, uber drivers are in fact drivers in lawful terms that these courts use. But if you notice in traffic court these Judges use the term driver to describe travelers and everyone else because there using policies and penal codes that were originally used and put into place for drivers and not travelers. This is due to our ignorance and their relentless extortion practices. Based on the mountain of facts it is clearly evident that they (the people governing our government) are now pursuing travelers under these policies without due process at Law extorting trillions and trillions of dollars from them on an annual basis not to mention every single natural person who goes before traffic court is in fact being tried under criminal court without due process of law and without all of the essential elements necessary for a fair and just trial which means the people are being process in these courts with no jury, no indictment papers, no qualified Judge (Article 3), no injured party and list goes on and on. When you really look into what's being done to the people which all of us are under duress by default these are grounds for class action lawsuits all across America and all over the world for that matter. But most people are in agreement to what's going on because when most people go before these traffic courts they NEVER object to court procedures not realizing that they can in fact OBJECT to these colorable (FRAUD) procedures. Most people don't even realize that their I.D.'s are in agreement with these facts simply because they agreed through their I.D.'s from the DMV to a privilege to "drive" and not the right to travel of which can never be taken away from anyone pursuant to your very own free-will to move about as you see fit to do so without any outside interference. You may be asking yourself how I know this to be true. One way is a person's intent. Your intent can be proving by the act itself. We all have the right to travel (liberty of locomotion in black's law dictionary 4$^{th}$ add). They use deceit to trick us into signing the driver license when we already have the right to locomotion. Deceit is also proven by their intent by the people by coerced into getting the driver instrument and following the quote unquote rules of the road. We are also threaten to be kidnapped and private property stolen if we don't produce this driver license. What we the people have to understand is that when you "apply" for a license you are filling out an application. The root word for application is to apply just like the root word for donation is to donate or the root word for belief is lie and so on. An application is "optional" in nature. It's no different when "applying" for a job. You don't have to apply for a particular job if you don't want to. So with that being said you don't have to apply for a license if you don't want to when you in fact already have the right to travel. They even have a form called the **DL142** that allows anyone to **CANCEL THEIR DRIVERS LICIENSE.** On one hand it is supposed to be optional but when you get on the road that's when it turns into something mandatory. When they created the DMV they should've issued travel ID's with no cost attached to it with the exception of the cost of material and ink applied to the I.D. But since their now all about robbing and extorting us they figured everyone must have one when applying is choice in the first place while traveling is a right. This could also be pointed out in court. When the people realize what are proper court procedures and what are not they will recognize immediately when a Judge is using unlawful procedures and can at that point object to them as soon as they recognize them. Until we the people realize that we in all traffic court cases (every single one of them) are in good standing with the law they will keep taking us through these unlawful procedures until we the people figure this thing out (the answers are in this book) and stand up. We must learn and understand that all policies and penal codes simply do not apply to natural persons only corporations (ALL CAPITOL LETTERS). But remember if you don't object they keep proceeding and ultimately they will find you guilty on whatever charges they have on you.

## Different Types of Traffic Tickets

Running a stop sign, making an illegal U-turn, failing to stop completely at stop sign, running a red light, changing lanes without proper signaling, driving a vehicle without properly functional turn signals & brake lights, no brake lights, driving without headlights, transporting an unsafe load in an unsafe manner, reckless endangerment, tinted windows violation, driving without a license, distracted driving, driving with use of a cell phone, busted tail light, texting and driving, illegally passing a school bus, child restraint violation, unlawful vehicle modifications, Neon under glow lighting violations, tail gating, no registration, cruising violation, crossing double yellow lines, driving on side walk, failure to obey sign, improper backing, following too closely, improper lights, fail to yield right of way, cutting in, blocking traffic, driving at zero mph, driving too fast for conditions, driving under the influence, no seat belt, etc.

Notice throughout this book that I don't really mention different types of violations simply because they do not apply to travelers not to mention there aren't any verified complaints filed although many of us have agreed to a license however it's all about your intentions. Most people who get behind the wheel intentions is not to conduct business from it.  Another reason why I don't mention them is because time and time again I've notice a pattern with people that get traffic tickets. I've noticed that we get caught up in the glamour of what actually happened (telling the story) from what the officer said to you noticing the officer(s) lying boldly in your face to whatever else happened during the traffic stop. Understand these simple yet powerful truths that if there isn't a verified complaint on file with the court and the plaintiff isn't present on the day of the Arraignment they have no case and it is truly irrelevant what you were charged with. Consider all traffic fines exactly the same and don't allow a cop, a judge, or anyone for that matter to confuse you in any way. Again when it comes to getting any traffic ticket the procedure and remedy is always the same. There may be one exception like a DUI and even with this charge it's still very similar to the rest of the bunch. Just treat it like all of the rest. These methods are also great for actual drivers who drive for a living. Before I lose anyone in what I'm trying to convey to you all is that first and foremost let me state for the record that I strongly believe in safety. I don't want people to go out and start running red lights because that would be foolish and possibly deadly on your part. These rules are set up in place for safety reasons for "drivers" which I am in agreement with however when these rules pore over onto travelers and used for extortion methods  that's when I have an issue with it. I think that they are good to follow but not falsely pulled over for a fake emergency and then citied to pay money at a later date because of it. Me personally I don't run red lights because I strongly believe in safe practices however if I were to run a red light unintentionally and I get pulled over and forced into a adhesion contract unwillingly and later forced to pay then I have a serious problem with it.

# *Chapter 3:*

## Straw-man vs. the Natural Person

I love pulling my I.D. out and asking people if the person on the I.D. is me and they always say yes right after looking at me and my photo ID. Then I state to them that it's not me. It is just a picture of (of meaning off or off of) me. Then I say that I'm me and I'm standing right here in front of you. For some it takes a minute or two to sink in. This is because most people are not aware that their I.D's are not a proper representation of their natural selves. Keep in mind when these statements are made that all law is specific and is detailed as much as possible. Think about this, you as a natural person will always be you and you will never expire even in death BUT your ID has an expiration date on it lasting on average about 4 years or so with some States giving your expiration date 10 years or more (Arizona being 1 of those States). A natural person is a living, breathing, thinking flesh and blood physical body. Now notice as the other 'person' is a Corporation which is a legal fiction or 'Artifice' created by a legal process that only have an existence on paper for its credibility which is your "name" is in all CAPITOL LETTERS but yet we were taught in elementary (elements) school that the 1st letter in your name is capitalized and the rest lower case. An example of this would be "John Doe" is the correct way. Not Doe, John, or John D., or J. Doe, or J. D., or JOHN DOE, or DOE JOHN, or any other variation expressed on paper as to who you are that ties to your natural self. This is an artificial man of straw, or straw-man. Do you think that the Department of Motor Vehicle (I believe are organize criminals that racketeer & extort daily) did this by accident? I think not, or better yet I know not. When you go before the tribunal (courts) and talk with these so-called Judges they literally view you in this light (straw man or corporation status) and their main objective is to extract revenue ($$$$$) from you as quickly and as efficiently as possible. The natural person has different rights within a court of law if that natural person is aware of their inalienable and or unalienable rights and EXERCISES them effectively. The natural person under common law is not subjected to all those policies, Statutes, ordinances, and penal codes if certain things are said in traffic court and put on the record even though most traffic courts are not recording. You can actually make and keep a record for yourself via cell phone or request that they record via motion requesting that they do so. By you getting a better understanding of it all and once you grasp this information you will be able to walk into a court room and easily beat any ticket that these policy enforcers (cops) throw at you. Have you ever notice that cops are quote unquote Law Enforcement but yet penal codes get pushed upon you and you rarely hear the words "you violated the law as it is stated within the Constitution" because in reality you never violated ANY LAW. I would respect the Police and their agencies from which they came from more so if they were honest and just say that they were policy enforcers and not Law Enforcement because there not really enforcing the law 90% of the time. It is of vital importance that you read this information over and over and over as it becomes easier and easier so that you have a clear understanding so that you know this information in order to get the full benefits of what is being conveyed to you. Just remember that the natural person that's linked to a Nation isn't subjected to pay all these fines that are based in penal codes and policies, only Corporations and "drivers" (anyone who is in agreement with this process) are subjected to them if they are in their proper person. May I suggest that you read this book at least 3-5 times to allow the information to truly sink in?

# *Chapter 4:*

## A Verified Complaint

This is in so many words what I'd like to call the **MISSING LINK** or **MISSING PUZZLE** piece to the confusion of those who are on the journey trying to figure out if they can either legitimately beat their ticket fines without it being based on a "technicality", getting lucky when the cop doesn't show up, or if they sense that something is just not right within the justice system. All laws make sense to virtually anyone. When they stop making sense it's no longer the law. Think of the law like gravity, IT NEVER CHANGES and when it does, it's no longer the law. Within the law of gravity anything that goes up will always come down*100%* of the time all day every day. The thing about driving and the rules that govern them is that they included everyone instead of it being properly implemented on only those who drove for a living. If the DMV was operating in accordance to the law they would have also allowed the people to get ***traveler ID's*** that wouldn't come with a charge or fee. They actually started making up driver rules for the road calling them penal codes and vehicle codes then tricked and forced the masses of the people into agreement with penal codes then convinced us that we as travelers should pay when driver codes were being violated partly because our forced identification is in agreement with it by lack of choice and they were successful at doing this partly because we the people in my opinion are under a belief system which doesn't challenge what is being told to them to verify what was said or what to believe. We either believe in Santa Clause, the Tooth Fairy, Jesus, the Easter Bunny, or some other made up fictitious entity. I'm not saying that people shouldn't have a belief system however we shouldn't just take what anyone is telling us as truth especially if there trying suck you financially dry. You should NEVER BELIEVE YOUR FINANCIAL ENEMY and just take their word for it. To assume that a person/system who is robbing you through an unfair process and getting away with it only because you don't know is being honest with you is absolutely INSANE. The truth about how to beat traffic tickets is being revealed through this book as more and more people are reading it and standing up and realizing that they have rights as natural persons that are protected and secured by the Constitution. I had a woman in court on Hill street in downtown L.A. tell me (based on her ignorance) that the Constitution doesn't apply in traffic court and I told her that it doesn't apply to her because she doesn't know how to apply it. The United States Constitution is an up to date and current contract that is probably more valid than any valid document that anyone of us currently holds. Every Judge that holds a seat in traffic court has taken an oath to uphold, preserve, and defend the Constitution against all enemies foreign and domestic. Now if you're paying attention I didn't say that they swore an Oath on all policies, penal codes, and statues. You may be asking yourself then why are they enforcing these codes & not the Constitution. And the answer is simple.....they don't make as much money from defending the Constitution as they would like to, they make money from enforcing codes which deviates from the Law AND it adds confusion to a relatively simple document (the Constitution) that makes it harder to cipher through and make sense of it all. Now let's get into this thing that's called ***a*** verified complaint and how it applies to you in traffic court and it will also show and prove how they have been extorting trillions of dollars from the people since its inception and how it's 1 big racketeering scheme because it doesn't co-inside with the way the courts are supposed to process you in hints Due Process of Law or what I'd like to call the process that is lawfully due to you.

Now let's say that someone breaks into your car. Soon after you find out you immediately call the police department. They send a squad car out and then they do what's called an investigation trying to figure out who, what, when, where, how, and why. They would ask you all sorts of questions like what time did you park your car, to what was missing from it, they may even dust for finger prints, to possibly asking your neighbors any questions that give them a possible lead. Now let's say that they find a finger print other than family members or yourself that they have in their criminal data base that leads them to a possible suspect. So now they know exactly who to go get. They would take their report back to the station where the Detectives would do a more thorough investigation on the matter until they feel based on the evidence that they are 100% sure that the person that popped up in their data base is in fact the person that actually committed the crime by either a confession or by an eye witness who saw that particular person. So from that point the Detectives would then send all of their paperwork which is also known as the complaint from the victim who's car got broken into over to the District Attorney's office. The District Attorney would then re-investigate what the Detectives discovered in the investigation to make sure that they go after the right person because in all criminal matters (Traffic Court is listed under criminal court) they try not to convict innocent people because they would be messing with someone's livelihood. So this is the reason that they go to great lengths to make sure that they truly indeed have the right person(s) involved in the matter. Now the complaint has gone through all of the chain of commands to the top which is the District Attorney's office. The only agency that can sign off on a criminal complaint is a District Attorney's office. And when they sign off on it after verifying that everything within the Detectives' investigations is true and valid, it then becomes what's called a VERIFIED COMPLAINT. Just like when you verify your own personal check by signing it. By the D.A. office signing off on this matter it also means that their responsible for this verified complaint being valid and just. Now this verified complaint is supposed to be started or originated from a victim or PLAINTIFF which is the same person. There also known as the injured party. This victim or plaintiff is supposed to be the very reason why you're in court in the 1st place. This is the procedure for any criminal case because Traffic Court is listed under criminal court (even though they say it's a different kind of crime and they call citations infractions). Although you might run into Traffic Court that may be listed under civil court. If this is done just remember that are supposed to produce a valid contract between 2 or more parties. If you've ever seen any court show like *Judge Mathis, Judge Judy, Divorce Court, or The People's Court there is* **ALWAYS 2 OPPOSING SIDES IN ALL MATTERS** or else whoever doesn't show or makes themselves present on the day of their scheduled court date would AUTOMATICALLY for fit their case and the Judge would rule in favor of the party who showed up. Now if you looked at the triangle in this book it clearly shows you a Judge, a Defendant, and the Plaintiff (the plaintiff is the person who four fits in the matter). In traffic court the triangle is broken........do you know why? It's because most people just believe whatever the Judges say as being true without challenging or questioning any information given to them. The triangle is broken because people are under a belief system and they are highly aware of this. And when you believe in something or someone you tend to not question it or them. I once told someone that it's actually 7 different ways (the way I count it) and not 3 that you can make a plea in traffic court based on rather or not there's a verified complaint on file with the court. You can plead guilty, not guilty, or no contest WITH a verified complaint or you can plead guilty, not guilty, no contest, or NO PLEA at all WITHOUT a verified complaint. It's actually impossible to make a plea in a case when the individual doesn't have a complaint from an actual person. They were shocked that they didn't know this and at the fact that the Judge did not tell them. But again why would anyone believe someone who is trying to take their money. You may be wondering as to why their able to get away with it. Well one reason is that we have forgotten the Law. If you don't know, they're not going to tell you and even more so they're not obligated to tell you. You must know.......you must bring it to their attention....otherwise there just going to assume that you are one of the many that believe you owe them and they are more than happy to accept your money. You also may be thinking "but why isn't getting a traffic ticket from a cop isn't a crime. Well the answer to this question is 3 fold. 1st and foremost intent and an act have to happen. Going back to the story where the person broke into the victim's car. He had a thought that he's going to break into that car. Then his thought (thought is intent) manifested into action and he went and did it. So now the crime is committed. He broke into the car and stole the stereo. This is in law what they call a legitimate crime. And in order *for something to be considered a crime there has to be a plaintiff, and with a plaintiff they would have to file a complaint, and with this complaint it would have to graduate into a verified complaint.* And the REVERSE is true. If there is no plaintiff, there cannot be a complaint, and without a complaint there can never ever be a verified complaint. So if the whole basis of this argument is because someone complained against you and they need to have a verified complaint to bring you into any court. This is essentially why the triangle is broken. See the game that their playing? It's a cold lie. But it's real. Now just think about all the things that were just explained to you. Now do you see why there's no plaintiff? Because if they bring in the plaintiff which by the way their never is in Traffic Court they would have to do the right thing but they don't and they know that you don't know and they're not going to tell you. Why? It's because the state of California is currently making well over 10-13billion dollars annually all the while over 18 million travelers in California are being sited annually. Now times that by however many more states there are give or take a few billion. It's simply big business folks.

# *Chapter 5:*

## 3 Steps In the Process of Traffic Court

1) **Status:** Nationality..........who are you? What Nation do you represent? Lawfully

**Types of Courts & types of Crimes**

2) **Jurisdiction/Venue** What territory do you have the Authority to impose Judicial powers? 3Parts
   a) Jurisdiction over the natural person (YOU)
   b) Jurisdiction over the matter at hand (your Citation/Bill of Attainder)
   c) Jurisdiction/Venue over the geographical territory (city & state)

3) **Adjudication:** The process of discussing the outcome of the alleged accusations (traffic ticket & cost). In an orderly & lawful manner

**Status**
**4 Types of Citizens**

1) **National; the highest ranking citizen, these are the indigenous aboriginal Moors and inhabitants of the land by heritage, bloodline, and lineage.**

2) **<u>Naturalized Citizen;</u> these are people who came here to become citizens through the Naturalization process (not to be confused with Nationalization).**
3) **<u>Subject;</u> this is where Corporations (folks who are not within their own rightful government) rest within the business of the UNITED STATES OF AMERICA INC., and ALL STATES under brand names such as Negros, blacks, Latinos, Creole, African Americans, coloreds, or any brand name that would take any person out of their Nationality.**
4) **<u>Aliens;</u> these are "foreigners" who will always remain as foreigners, while residing here in the Americas.**

Status is the standing, state, or condition (correct or incorrect) of an individual; the rights (or lack thereof) obligations, capacities, and incapacities that assign an individual to a given class. An example of this would be using the term status in reference to a legal state of being an infant which by the way is someone with an unsound mind or very little to no comprehension, a ward which is a slave, or a prisoner, as well as in reference to a person's social standing in the community. Part of a natural person having the proper status is being under a Nation via having a Nationality. Even a more important part of your status is link directly to your estate. A huge example of this would be the so called African Americans, Afro Americans, Negros, or blacks who are Moors pursuant to their Authentic and true Nationality (being black hold no Nationality which in turn leaves these people in a very vulnerable position for abuse) in the United States of North America (and abroad) claiming their land and property (houses, gold, metals, resources, etc.) back. As "African American" they waive the right to self-government and indigenous rights by admitting and agreeing to that. I believe Jessie Jackson coined the phrase "African American" (made popular) knowing that this made up Nationality doesn't have a National flag. A famous case named Dred Scott v. Sandford in 1857 will help you guys further understand this concept. All these things that were done and is still being done is to take the indigenous people out of their natural, political, social, and status positions in order for Europeans to rule and dominate here in the Americas because it's all about your position and where you stand in certain key venues. Here are some of the names that America and the original inhabitants were called before our so called modern time which simply meant "land in the West". Americans, Amurricans, Amurrukans, Amurikans, Al Mauri'kans, Al Moro'cans, Morl'cans, Maurs, Mors, Moors, Murrs, Muurs. To further help you understand where I'm coming from you can look up books on Amerigo Vespucci and Publius Cornelius Scipio Africanus. It was also never called India simply because this land is not India. Back on topic....by these people not having and claiming a Nationality would also means a breakup from the link or lineage that they once or originally had with their direct human family aka indigenous bloodline and ancestors. By these people not having a Nationality is essentially making them "non- descendible". In other words land, property, precious items from family members, etc. cannot be passed down to their children and their children's children and so on and so forth without the government having a say so in the matter. This would also leave them open to abuse (which is presently happening) of their land, property and misleading from the fraudulent misinformation like mortgages, contracts, the law, etc. If or when these people become aware of this crucial and powerful piece of information and vigorously act on it we will see the biggest transfer of land and property wealth in modern day history. It will be like each of them winning a huge power ball lottery winnings. Believe it or not some people think that when one becomes aware of their vast estate and claim what is already theirs by bloodline and birthright that they are robbing individuals, corporations, or businesses based off of their severe level of ignorance. This is because it signifies the condition or a circumstance in which the owner stands with in regards to his/her land/property. Someone with an ignorant mind set doesn't understand that Nations represent the ***LAND*** that one stand on.

And in this case by North America and its over seers are in a position of operating and maintaining "stolen land" and property from the original landlords/ or owners who are native indigenous peoples here on this vast estate that we now call the United States of America.

Here's what **Edward Wilmot Blyden** had to say at his speech he gave in July of 1877 prior to Noble Drew Ali gracing us with his much needed presence to awaking the so-called Negroes/African Americans of North America of their much needed Nationality.

"Nationality is an ordinance of nature. The heart of every true Negro yearns after a distinct and separate Nationality".

"We shall never receive the respect of other races until we establish a powerful Nationality. We should not content ourselves with living among other races simply by their permission or their endurance as Africans live in this Country. A well-established African Nationality is the most direct and efficient means of securing respectability and independence for the African race".

The so called African Americans were the 1st inhabitants here long before any other group of people and thus making them sole owners of this vast estate stretching as far as from Alaska, all of Canada, on down to all of the Americas North, Middle, South, including all of the joining islands, etc. Although they have no problem sharing parts of various landmasses. Status can also affect your freedoms, liberties, rights of travel in various ways. With proper status remedy can be giving to one whose rights have been violated in a court of law. This is why it is of vital importance to zoom in on law and jurisdiction and letting that be the focal point to address. In traffic court most of these judges don't have the proper status to engage with you within the court nor is this a priority to them. In all honesty I think that they could care less based on what I've heard personally from conversations with them for what I believe is of fraud purposes.

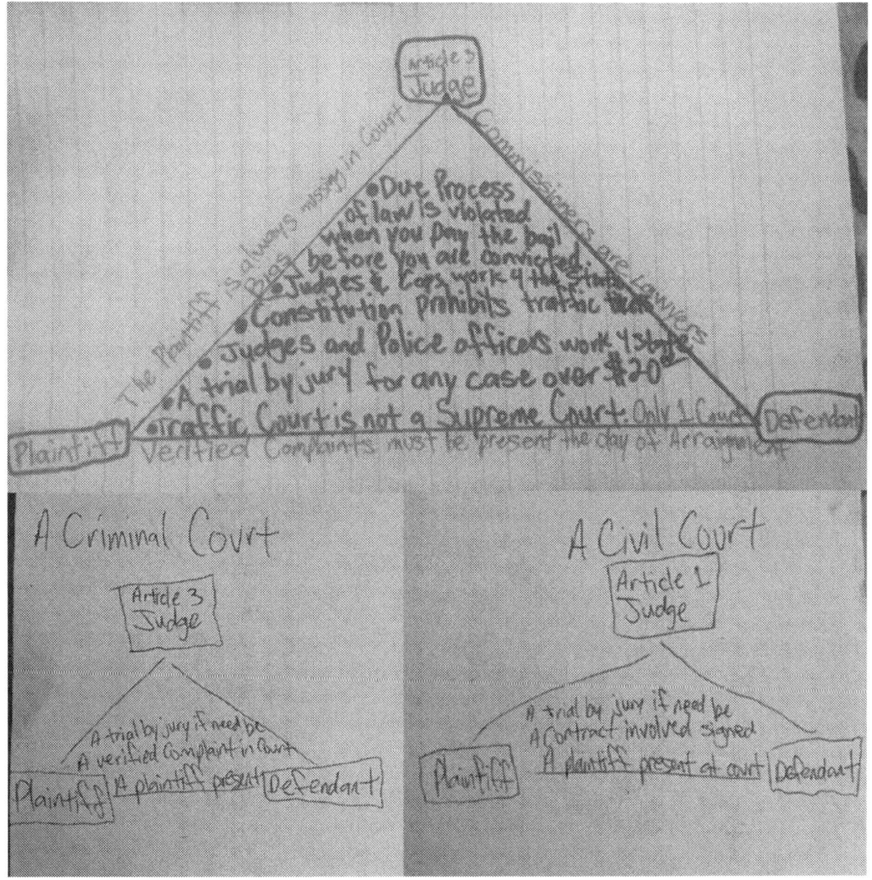


**Types of Courts & types of Crimes**

There are truly only **<u>2</u>** types of court: **<u>Criminal court</u>** & **<u>Civil court</u>** **(TRAFFIC COURT IS LISTED UNDER CRIMINAL COURT).** The Judge is in fact aware of what type of court you're in, either **<u>criminal court</u>** or **<u>civil court</u>**. In a **CRIMINAL** Tribunal ***(Tri means 3 sides or angles),*** for a **<u>crime</u>** to be proven, there must be certain(usually 5 elements) key elements of a **<u>crime</u>**: an "***<u>injured party</u>***" (1)present before they can proceed forward, a "**<u>witness</u>**" (2)for the alleged **crime** you have committed against the injured party, your "**<u>criminal intent</u>**" (3)of the alleged crime, a **"concurrence"** (4)of the alleged **crime** and a **"causation"** (5)of the alleged **crime.** All these afore mentioned elements must be present and proven before a JURY and there must be a PROSECUTOR present before the court can proceed**.** In other words there would be 3 essential elements that will be present which is a complaint (1),a sworn affidavit with the complaint (2) and an injured party that actually filed the complaint (3).This will be your 1st hint that you are in a fraudulent courtroom. Now of course the Judge can't and will not be honest with you in their fraudulent disposition, because their 1st obligation is to the business they work for, when in fact on the other hand their 1st obligation is to enforce and defend both Constitutions, of which they have taken a sworn oath/affirmation on to do so. When you are in a court room remember that all judges are **assuming and presuming** that you don't know your rights nor do you care to exercise them. So it becomes your job and duty to wake them up to your awareness to what you know. They all are (judges, clerks, cops, etc.) civil servants which means that they work for you which also indicates who's really the boss in the courtroom. And all criminal and civil cases must be tried in a **Supreme Court of justice, of which there is but 1 presiding judge.** Remember all traffic courts are Ministerial, Colorable (unlawful), or both. These are what I consider fake or fraudulent courts. These courts are paternity court, moral court, traffic court, parking enforcement court, and divorce court in which I've seen mostly on television. The very nature and true meaning of the word ***"TRAFFIC"*** has absolutely nothing to do with a natural person(YOU) being brought inside of that particular courtroom simply because you were not dealing with any type of commercial business, any trading, no merchandise, bills, and no money whatsoever during your time of **travel**. This is only applied to drivers by DEFINITION like **truck drivers**, **pizza delivery drivers**, **taxi drivers, limo drivers,** yard goat drivers, etc. It is very important for you to know how to, or how not to interface with all of these unlawful procedures and Judges. All Judges MUST be held to the Law, no exceptions because they've taken an oath and signed a contract that binds them to both Constitutions.

## JURISDICTION

Jurisdiction is the courts power and ability to hear a case between 2 or more parties. Courts usually based their concerns from 2 jurisdictions. The 1st is personal jurisdiction and the 2ndone is subject matter jurisdiction. It's important to understand what jurisdiction is because if you're thinking about or planning on filing a lawsuit it'll help you figure out what court you're going to file it in ultimately speeding up the process. Now with personal jurisdiction this is having jurisdiction over the 2 parties involved in the case then you (the plaintiff) file suit against another party or defendant that defendant must have certain contacts with the State in which you file suit. For example the defendant must either live in the State that you are suing him or her in or have some type of business or benefit from the State in order for the court to have personal jurisdiction over the defendant. However one of interesting things about personal jurisdiction is that it could be waived. So let's say that a court initially did not have jurisdiction over a person the courts can gain jurisdiction by the person waiving their rights. With that being the situation or case that defendant has waived any and all future challenges to the courts personal jurisdiction. Now the 2nd type of jurisdiction that a court can have is subject matter jurisdiction. This jurisdiction is different than personal jurisdiction being that it is the jurisdiction over the different types of cases that courts can hear. One thing to notice about this type of jurisdiction is that subject matter jurisdiction cannot be waived. If a court were to enter in a judgment without having subject matter jurisdiction that judgment is not enforceable in any way, shape, or form. Now the vast majority of courts have the authority to hear many cases however there are some instances in which the court would not have subject matter jurisdiction. An example of this would be a criminal court. Subsequently the 3rd component is adjudication which is the ruling of a case matter. Time also plays a vital role in the courts power and ability to render a verdict in a case. The statute of limitations defines a time limit within which the prosecution must file criminal charges. Someone at any time thereafter the crime has been committed. Once the clock runs out within a particular time frame for a particular offense a person cannot be convicted thereafter. This statute of limitation is limited to certain crimes. This is in ***Title 18 U.S. Code 3161 under time limits and exclusions***. A criminal court only has jurisdiction to hear criminal matters. So if you wanted to sue Wal Mart for a defective product that you brought from there you wouldn't be able to get your case heard in a criminal court for processing and remedy because it falls under civil suits being that it was a verbal contract and no bodily harm of any kind. The reason that traffic court doesn't have jurisdiction in any way whatsoever is because a valid case has to hold the elements to even be suitable to be heard and to be moved forward for possible conviction by law. When it comes to traffic court there is never a verified complaint on file with the court, nor is there a plaintiff in the matter, there was never a legitimate crime in the matter to begin with, and therefore should never even be presented for prosecution not to mention every person's car on the road doesn't fit the weight limit of these commercial vehicles. These commercial vehicles weight are set or marked at about 8,000 lbs. or more which isn't dealing with any common cars because none of the cars on the road today fit that weight description. A tractor trailer is roughly 12,500 lbs. pending on if it is a day cab or sleeper bed.

## CLEVER USE OF LANGUAGE/ADJUDICATION

This clever use of language and intimidation used by these judges and others is what I'd like to call ***verbal judo***. Keep this in mind that Names are corporate entities or businesses; Noble titles are applied to Natural living Human being's. A corporation like Burger King.......this would be the NAME of that particular business. A verbal act of telling a judge your status will separate you from being in a pro se or Corporate status into a proper and legal standing otherwise known as being In Propia Persona (pro per) Sui Juries & that you are a Natural person In Full Life meaning you literally go from being a business or property that they can extract money from, to being one's own proper self-possessing full social and civil rights while continuing in both physical and civil existence. If a natural human being states their title on the record, Policies and Penal Codes simply do not apply to that title, because they only apply to Corporations and or drivers. If a Judge asks someone for their ADDRESS, know that they are trying to gain Jurisdiction over that Natural person because what their really asking is do that natural person owns that Address, and by people not really knowing what the Judge intentions are, people answer these questions without thinking that the Judge could possibly be up to no good in their tactful and sneaky policy ways. The post office is the one who really owns addresses, not you.... remember, they are a business and you are there only because they seek to make money off of you, not because you violated any Law, and if this were so you would have all the elements (verified complaint, papers, a jury, a prosecutor, an injured party, etc.) a criminal courtroom would have but they don't. According to the Law A NOT GUILTY PLEA in terms of what they're writing tickets for, in fact means a human being is admitting Jurisdiction when these Judges ask something like "you were pulled over on this day and giving a citation by officer John Doe and was giving a ticket on citation #P47776 do you understand"?......What the Judge is really asking you is **WILL YOU STAND UNDER IN TERMS OF WHAT I'M TELLING YOU?**....or are you willing to submit under our unlawful tactics freely? To understand is also a verbal contract to something. Meaning it's just a choice like when you go to a tire shop and they ask you if you want chrome rims or not. It is simply a choice and you don't have to choose anything if you don't want to especially in a courtroom when they are not providing you with a verified complaint.

When a non-Article 3 (Administrator or Actor/Actress) judge asks you a question and its fashioned this way always keep in mind that they are using tactical tricks to get you to agree to something that you may not fully understand. When this is done ask them to explain it, and when they start talking about the policy or penal code that was violated immediately ask the Judge what section within the Constitution is that in because you don't see that part.........then ask if they took their Oath on something else because they're coming up with stuff you've never heard or seen within the Constitution. I remember my very first time going before a Judge asking him if there was a verified complaint on file with the courts and he said that the ticket is the complaint. Do not fall for this bold face lie. The ticket is not the complaint. They use this a lot so be sure to ask them if the ticket/red light camera ticket/etc. has all of the information from the plaintiff signed off from a District Attorney's office. Please know this truth for the truth will set "your pockets free". A real Article 3 Judge must prove their authority within a criminal venue (only if you demand proof) by possessing something that's called a Delegation of Authority Order (D.O.A.O) issued from Congress. If this is not present on the day that you make your special or private appearance they are unlawful better known as a FRAUD. Also Jurisdiction must be proven for the record. I recently discovered that Traffic Court Judges known as Commissioners, Referees, and Magistrates are deemed as incompetent within the law? Why? Simply because they practice that which is other than the law and that it doesn't stem from the Constitution. Go figure. **www.goodbyetrafficticket.com**

# *Chapter 6:*

## The Arraignment Process

These processes are not complicated provided that you get familiar with just a few and key **LAWFUL DEFINITIONS** and apply them. Tap into and focus on what you can do (going over this information until you have a very good understanding of it) verses what you cannot do. The definition of easy (in my opinion based on proven facts) is **something that you can do**. But at the same time it's easy **not to do**. With that being said and established if you are reading this book know that you can beat your "***traffic ticket***" with the help of this information at the arraignment hearing. Now sometimes it can get a little tricky only because different "Judges" have different responses when it comes to a person being well informed about court procedures at an arraignment (which is fairly basic). I have narrowed them down to just a few so that you don't get confused or thrown off from the goal at hand which is ***beating your traffic ticket free and clear***. Now the 1st one is after the conversation is flowing between you and the judge and after you have questioned them on their position they may get frustrated and slightly angry with you for speaking law and making sure he/she is doing their job properly and lawfully. I've been in situations and seen situations that ended up with me and others getting kicked out and rushed out of the court room. If this is done know that the judge is also kicking your case out as well and not just you AND it's also done in my opinion to create a diversion and throw the people off as to confuse them and so that the people do not and will not pick this information up. Now let's say that you're called up by the Judge and they speak on your issue like you violated penal code such and such I find you guilty, do you want to pay for violating this code or do you want to make a plea. Most people that go into a court room don't realize what exactly is the Judge's duties are when you approach the bench. The lawful definition that's in the law books is ***a public officer, appointed to preside and to administer the law in a court of justice; the chief member of a court, and charged with*** **THE CONTROL OF PROCEEDINGS AND TO ANSWER ANY LAWFUL QUESTIONS.** Now an **arraignment** is calling the defendant to the bar of the court, to answer the accusation contained in the indictment. **Indictment** papers is an accusation in writing found and presented by a grand jury, legally convoked and sworn, to the court in which it is impaneled, charging that a person therein named has done some act, or been guilty of some omission, which, by Law, is a public offense, punishable on indictment. **A Plea** is a suit or action. To be made aware of someone's actions or suits between 2 parties. The answer in which the defendant in an action at Law makes to the plaintiff's declaration. A **plaintiff** is a person who brings an action; the party who complains or sues in a personal action and is so named on the record. A **defendant** is the person defending or denying; the party against whom relief or recovery is sought in an action or suit. There's also a 3 part pyramid (***TRIBUNIAL***) to the structure of a court room in terms of the process. The 1$^{st}$ one is at the top of the pyramid which is the Judge/ Commissioner/Referee. The 2$^{nd}$ sits at the right bottom which is the defendant (YOU), and last but not least is the plaintiff at the bottom left of the pyramid. Now if you're paying attention almost **ALWAYS THE PLAINTIFF IS MISSING BECAUSE THERE IS NO PLAINTIFF WHICH MAKES THE CHARGES THAT'S BEING BROUGHT AGAINST YOU UNPROSECUTABLE** . Now that we have clarity on these lawful definitions and the way a court room process works you will clearly see and understand how to easily beat a ticket (all traffic tickets fall in this category) in traffic court. Now let's begin. **Judge**: John Doe how do you plea? **YOU**: well your I cannot make a plea because I have not received the plaintiff's declaration, or you can say your honor is there a verified complaint on file with the courts and is the plaintiff showing up today because without this plaintiff I would assume that you will be dismissing this case pursuant to discovery laws. **Judge:** Excuse me....if you received a traffic ticket that would indicate to me that you are in fact aware of these charges and that the ticket would be the verified complaint at this point. **YOU:** what am I making a plea on? There's no verified complaint on file with the court nor is there a plaintiff present today sir. **Judge:** Well I'm going to make a plea for you of guilty/not guilty/or (most likely he'll make a "not guilty plea" for you)**. YOU**: Objection, are you practicing law from the bench sir? **You:** you cannot make a plea for me in this court for what you are doing is a deliberate act of unlawful procedures that are being force upon me under color of law under title 18 United States Law**. JUDGE:** Get out of my court room now.....the bailiff(s) would more than likely at this point escort you out of the court room. **YOU:** Just calmly gather your paper work and leave the court room. If there is no plaintiff they have no case and it's really that simple. Just remember when the Judge kick you out it also means that he's kicking your case out.......get it. And make sure that you do a follow up on that case to make sure they dismissed it. Or it could go another way; the Judge might try to gain jurisdiction over you by getting you to agree to your corporation ID card or driver's license. The Judge might say something along these lines........."Can you state your name? Your response should be objection; I don't have a name I am......then state (what you know to be your name) what your mamma gave you. And in many cases the Judge will try to throw you off by repeating this question over and over and over. When this is done keep repeating the same response over and over until the Judge gives in. It is because when you say "my", it means that you possess something because "my" is possessive.

So in essence if you own "your name" (notice your ID is in ALL CAPITOL LETTERS) then you're obligated (your ID represents a Business) to whatever they put on you in terms of any type of financial strain because your ID is not you, it's a business (as crazy as it may sounds). And a name doesn't mean what we think it means in common everyday terms. A name in law that these courts go by means that you're simply a corporation/business (like McDonald's or Starbucks). Now of course we are not manufactured goods but if we don't object (to go against what they say based on the Law) they keep on proceeding and by us not knowing/realizing that you not only have the right to object to these unlawful procedures but when they don't uphold the law you also have the right to literally sue them(Article 3 Judges) in another court when they don't honor their oath(ask for a real Judge if there not upholding the law and their obligations) of office which is in fact being breached on a daily basis all across the U.S. The consequence for these folks (Judges) breaching their oath is death by hanging. That's to let everyone know that they are supposed to take this stuff very seriously. However as you all already know these things have been compromised. Or the Judge could say something like if you were to ask him to produce his documents (D.O.A.O or Article 3) if the Judge says that they don't have them there telling you in so many words that YOU ARE IN THE WRONG PLACE. And so what you could do is just simply say "your honor I'm sorry I believe I am in the wrong place.........am I free to go"? Not always but in many cases they will let you walk right on out of there. Or if the Judge gets quiet on you it simply means their thinking of what to say next or they just don't know how to respond, when they do this again let them know that you believe that you are in the wrong place and are you free to go based on default and a lack of due process of law? If they start playing games with you or act like they don't know what you're talking about this is the perfect time to start asking for documents that they don't have like his/her performance bond, etc. When it's clear that they cannot answer your question state to them that based on their oath of office, a lack of due process, and based on default I demand that you dismissed this suit before you on grounds of Law under Article 1 section 11 of the Constitution of the State of California (or whatever State you reside in). Let's be clear of one thing which was already mentioned that they don't want people knowing this information so keep in mind that in most cases they will just kick you out of the court room which means that their kicking your case out as well. And try to remember to end all of your sentences in "for the record". And if at all possible try and have a recorder of your own because they're not recording cases in traffic court (hint hint). And that is pretty much how you beat a traffic ticket at the arraignment. It's actually better to beat the ticket at this point because you're going over a lot less information than at your court trial. And whenever you start to think at any time (which I doubt) that they are not violating the law just ask yourself this one simple question......if you were making 10-13 billion dollars a year would you tell people the truth about how they really don't owe on their traffic tickets if it was your company OR would you just keep getting paid until they woke up, figured it out, and demand for themselves proper procedures at law? I have an idea of what your answer probably is but either way and at the end of the day these people (Judges and cops) have taken an oath to defend the Constitutions and not spit on it so to speak. For all those reading these few pages of information you now have some valuable tools that you and your family can use for the rest of your life and not ever pay for another traffic ticket again......EVER. Good luck and good study to all those who enforce the Constitution.

## --IF YOUR AFFIDAVITS/MOTIONS ARE DENIED REPEAT THE FOLLOWING—

**When Judges deny your affidavits or motions you can say "can you please state the finding of facts and conclusions of Law as to WHY my motions/writ/affidavits are being denied? For the record**

## ARRAIGNMENT SCRIPT #1 NEGATIVE

**Judge:** How do you plea?

**You:** Have you read my documents that I submitted to the courts your honor?

**Judge:** What documents? I don't have any information on whatever you submitted. Do you have a copy of what you've submitted?

**You:** Yes I do. (Submit your documents to the bailiff)

**Judge:** Give me a few moments here while I take a look at these documents (going over your documents on the spot). Or they might say give me about 15 minutes while I review these documents in my chambers.

**Judge:** I've reviewed your documents and even though there are some valid points in your paperwork I'm still going to need you to make a plea.

**You:** Your honor is there a verified complaint on file with the court from a plaintiff coming out of a District Attorney's office for the record? Also ***is the PLAINTIFF coming today*** because if not I would appreciate it for you to dismiss this suit due to a lack of a verified complaint, a plaintiff, and a lack of jurisdiction for the record.

**Judge:** I'm not trying to hear all that; my job is to take people's plea…… that is it. Now how do you plea?

**You:** I want to make a plea as long as I'm being lawfully presented with a verified complaint by a plaintiff from a District Attorney's office for the record.

**Judge:** Go to the clerk's window & get a court date.

**You:** Your honor I would like to also ask for an O.R. (this means to be released on your **O**wn **R**ecognizance) giving the fact that I showed up today and I'm not a flight risk or anything of that nature for the record.

**Judge:** Alright I'll waive the bail amount this time. Go down the hall to the clerk's window to get your court date for your trial.

**You:** Thank you your honor.

**Caution:** it is ultimately at your discretion to make a plea or not. You don't have to make a plea without a verified complaint. It's within their rules however be prepared for them to play the game with you as far as trying to drag you back into court and having you start all over because this is what they do. Trickery at its finest.

## ARRAIGNMENT SCRIPT #1 POSITIVE

**Judge:** How do you plea?

**You:** Your honor did you read or review my documents?

**Judge:** yes I have.

**You:** Have you reached a verdict based on the evidence that I submitted?

**Judge:** Yes I have, based on the evidence that you've submitted your case is being dismissed. Sometimes the Judge will call your name before proceedings even begin and tell you that your case is being dismissed.

**You:** Thank you your honor. From that point just gather up your documents and quietly leave the courtroom.

## --IF YOUR AFFIDAVITS/MOTIONS ARE DENIED REPEAT THE FOLLOWING—

**When Judges deny your affidavits or motions you can say "*can you please state the finding of facts and conclusions of Law as to WHY my motions are being denied? For the record.* Sometimes they will say oh because I have the Authority to do so and if this is said your response should be "great, *may I* see *your Delegation of Authority Oder issued to you by Congress of the United States Republic North America for the record?* This is their license to run the court under the judicial powers.**

# *Chapter 7:*

## My Encounter with a Cop on Hill Street

*I remember it almost like it was yesterday when I went to court on Hill Street in downtown Los Angeles in June of 2013 sitting in the room on the 4th floor a bit irritated from listening to the recording that the courts have masterfully shuffled like a deck of cards of what your rights are and it not being detailed and simplified as it should. So finally after the recording had stopped an Officer began explaining what our options were in order to help speed up the process. So after about a minute or so had passed he starts talking about bail and how it applies to the people and pretty much giving them direction as far as how to go about paying the bail amount after their plea was made. So after he finished up lying to the people about this bail process he asked the audience did anyone have a question. When I looked around I noticed that no one had raised their hand. It was almost like mostly everyone in their on that day seemed very irritated and just wanted the whole process to be done with already. So when I noticed that no one was interested in asking him any questions I decided to put a little heat on the Cop and ask him one question so that the people in the courtroom can have a little light shed on their issues and possibly wake up to the lie that's starring them right in the face. So after I rose my hand he ask me what was my question. I said sir do you mean to tell me that bail does in fact applies in this matter? Then he said yes but what's your question though? I then said sir according to penal code 19.6 it clearly states and I quote Infractions are crimes not punishable by imprisonment so in other words I can't go to jail for this as long as I show up on my court date. He then stated okay..........but what's your point? I said sir what I'm saying is if you know the real and accurate definition of what bail means and to make a long story short and I was talking fast because it seemed like he wanted to cut me off and just rush me through my question but I continued by saying sir bail is basically to get somebody out of jail or it's to prevent them from going to jail, and again infractions are crimes not punishable by imprisonment so what I'm trying to convey to you sir is that bail doesn't even apply in this matter so what are you talking? Then he looked a bit puzzled and then said oh......you don't know what you're talking about.......you've just confused yourself. I then said I'm not confused and actually I think that your confused sir because I know the definition....in fact I read the Black's Law Dictionary every other day. And he immediately cut me off and from that point he had his eye on me so long story short as other people were going through the proceedings, waiving their rights and giving them up. Shortly thereafter he came by where I was sitting and told me that my case was being transferred to the 5th floor. And I'm thinking to myself this guy is up to something because out of every body case which it was about 40 something people in court that my case was the only one being transferred. So I pretty much had whatever type of attitude like I'll deal with anybody. So I go upstairs to the 5th floor and noticed that this Judge's attitude was very rude, cold, and just outright disrespectful. He was literally shooting people down, not allowing them to bypass the bail amount, not reducing anyone's fine, sending them to collections, I mean you name it and he was doing it. So as the line starts moving as I get closer and closer to the front, he says my name with an attitude Gregory Garrett? I approach the bank I mean the bench, and I stated on the record that I am appearing specially and not generally and in the middle of me saying these things he very boldly cuts me off......"I DON'T WANNA HEAR ALL THAT.....HOW DO YOU PLEA"? I said sir I wouldn't cut you off so I would appreciate if you didn't cut me off. And right then and there we got in to it. So after going back and forth with him for about a minute or so he asks me again........"How do you plea"? Then I said very quickly "sir before I make a plea is there a verified complaint on file with the court from an actual plaintiff coming out of a District Attorney's office because if not I would ask of you to dismiss this case based on default and a lack of a verified complaint"? Then he said.....what on earth are you talking about very loudly then he told me very aggressively to sit down. What you want to remember folks and understand is that they don't want this type of information to get out in my opinion and will do pretty much any and everything within their power to protect their multibillion dollar industry. But needless to say after he sat me down and allowed everyone else to go before me and got them to consent or agree with him that they owed something that they didn't have i.e. Gold and silver he stood me back up and told me to slow it down on the road (yes I was going above the speeding limit that they suggest to us not to go over) because it's a safety issue on the road and he also told me that my case is being dismissed. I had to pull teeth it seemed like so to speak but he honored his Oath reluctantly and threw the case out. As long as you're willing to challenge them with courage and truth they are more likely to stand down and grant you a dismissal which by the way is the lawful thing to do. And remember too that they will purposely speak over you or while you're talking because if you don't get your entire question out of your mouth they don't have to answer it......get it? But again this works only when we bring up truth and speak up. I'm merely speaking on my own experiences however I have personally seen this work for a great number of other people as well.*

# *Chapter 8:*

## What I've Said @ Court Trial

***WHAT I'VE SAID @ COURT TRIAL***

After the cop gives his testimony & the Judges allows you to speak you could immediately OBJECT to the cops' entire testimony by saying.........*"**Objection my honor, those are facts not entered into evidence, the only thing that's in my court case file is a citation** (*which is just a promise to appear*) **and the evidence that I submitted therefore I am unable to properly prepare myself with a fair and just defense" FTR".*** (See what the Judge says) You can also say.....***for the record my honor if this is criminal I must also OBJECT because there's no injured party or plaintiff in this manner since this suit/case is considered a crime.*** (See what the Judge says) If he tries to dispute that just let the Judge know that from your understanding based on law Traffic Court is listed under criminal court. *You have to keep in mind that Commissioners or Referees are just people. They speak English just like you do, they put 1 pants leg on 1 at a time JUST LIKE YOU DO, they eat, breath, sleep, just like you do, so in essence it's really nothing to fear but fear itself because they can't put you in jail for knowing what law really is . The Law is OVERWELMINGLY in your favor or on your side in terms of the colorable procedures that are being implemented in traffic court which by the way is unlawful for the sole purpose of making money that's not on one* *accord with the Constitution. So your job is to expose that through paper work and if need be speak on certain issues like that verified complaint and plaintiff and get you out from that fraudulent position that their trying to force upon you. Now keep in mind you do not.......I repeat you do not want to get into a long debate with the Judge/Commissioner/Referee simply because they are very good at using* ***clever use of language*** otherwise known as ***verbal*** **judo**. So *the best thing you can do to rid yourself of them tricking you off subject or paying this fraudulent debt is to not allow them to take you off of the subject that you're speaking on. Now make sure that you are prepared before you enter the court room. Have your recorder and or your cell phone and hit record right before they call your name so that you can have a record of the proceedings because they are probably not recording the crimes that they commit daily. The 1*[st] *thing you could say after the Judge has spoken and allow you to speak that* **you are a natural person and that you are in full life** ***for the record***. *1*[st] *(this piece here is optional) say* **for the record can you please provide me with adequate proof from the department of State and from a Federal court that you have stepped inside of a Federal Court room in front of a Federal Jury and provided them with adequate proof that I'm a corporation?** *Next if the cop gave his testimony before you and when it's your turn to speak object to the cop's entire testimony because you didn't know what he was going to say for his information wasn't placed in evidence with the court so that you can prepare for a proper defense for the record.* **YOU: My honor I received this information in the mail** *(the mail with the bail amount that they send to your home when you get a ticket)* **and it says right here "people of the State of California vs. John Doe (your name in all capital letters) guy here now this fanatically sounds like my name but it's not, and for the record this Corporation is not me. And so I came any way because I know that certain police officers have a tendency to detain and arrest people on the street......and so I came here under threat, duress, and coercion under private appearance to answer relative to this so that no assumptions of jurisdiction are**

**made without me contesting to some fraudulent jurisdiction. Are you aware of that Judge because I want that for the record? And so if there are any future correspondences with me can you please see to it that your private corporation corrects this matter so that they don't assume that I'm some corporation because I'm a natural person for the record. And I also wanted to make a special note for the county clerk that this is truly a fraudulent instrument and I don't expect any more of these in the mail, and if they continue to come I'm saying on the record that this is nothing more than an attempt to extort from me and to intimidate me under color of law and Judge you have an obligation to see to it that this doesn't take place now or in the near future so can you please take care of this for me by dismissing this suit in its entirety for the record?** *Judge's response: (whatever that may be)The Judge might try to discredit what you have just said so if the Judge doesn't dismiss the citation right then and there you can also come at them another way. Let's say the Judge says I'm not dismissing your citation at this point so we will continue with the case matter here. Ok after he gets done talking and possibly the cop also when it is your turn to speak you can say this........* **YOU: Excuse me my honor you're talking about the subject matter or the subject before the court and status has not been established and placed on the record for the record and I would like for you to do that now.** *Next after his response if he doesn't dismiss it you then can say* **"my honor at this time I would like to challenge the Jurisdiction of this court for the record** *and remain* **silent** *until he responds and answers the question proving the jurisdiction of the court with some form of paperwork. If he doesn't answer the question repeat your question and let him or her know that they have to show proof by law and that they've taken an oath on the Federal Constitution. Also let them know from time to time that you do not waive any of your rights at any time during these proceedings and command the Judge of this court at all times to uphold his or her obligations on their sworn in oath of office. If for some reason he gets passed that you can say.....* **my honor may I see your certificate of a**

**delegation of authority order issued to you by congress of the United States Republic of North America FTR?** *In most cases they almost always never get pass this point but again if for whatever reason they pass this point you can then begin reading your questions for the cop & towards the end read the supreme court case rulings. And of course if they find their way pass that and unlawfully find you guilty just go straight to the clerk's window and fill out the* ***appeal paperwork*** *in a timely fashion. And remember* ***you have the ability to*** *go in there and* ***SMASH THAT TICKET.*** These are merely suggestions. If for any reason you don't feel comfortable you can always just stick to the trial questions for the cop and you should be fine if you choose to. I actually suggest to all beginners to only deal with the trial questions for the cop.

# *Chapter 9:*

## Trial Questions Judges

### QUESTION FOR THE JUDGE/MAJESTRATE

When participating in a court Tribunal, **for the record (FTR) is a phrase used at the end of each statement or sentence.**

1) What is your full name FTR?
2) Are you a Judge, Magistrate, Commissioner, Protemt, or Referee FTR?
3) Do you have and hold a valid sworn Oath of Office that is required of you by the State of California (or whatever State they reside in) and the United States Republic North America FTR?
4) Do you have valid hazardous bonds as well as other bonds that's also required of you by the Constitution as well as by Law FTR?

A) You could ask the Judge have they taken an oath to support, enforce, & preserve the Constitution for the United States **Republic** (**Democracy** is a **Fraud**) North America **FTR?**
B) Ask the Judge are they an **ARTICLE 3** Judge and does he/she have proof of their performance bond within the Constitutional fold of Government......**FTR?**

C) You could state to the Judge that they're asking for a payment that you do not have according to the Constitution which states that nothing but **gold and silver is lawful money** and that you've never been issued any **real money** so how do you expect me to pay this debt back in a lawful manner?.....**FTR**

D) Ask the Judge to see his **Delegation of Authority Order (DOAO)** issued to him by Congress of the United States Republic North America. FTR

**E)** **Article** 7 of ***the Bill of Rights*** states **ANY SUIT** in controversy at common Law(Constitution) ***that exceeds $20.00*** that **<u>you have a right to a trial by jury</u>** of your National Peers and that you don't see any of your Nation of peers present.....**FTR** **<u>so demand it.</u>**

**F)** **A judge almost always** jumps to the adjudication process. This means the Judge will start talking about what a Human being owes on the citation, this is irrelevant. Any judge's statement can be **<u>objected/objection</u>** in a court hearing, on grounds of lack of due process or proper proceeding's ("**<u>on grounds of law").</u>**

G) A judge cannot lawfully proceed with a hearing, if certain documents have not been placed and filed properly with the court. Any human being that assumes authority to possess judicial powers shall and must derive authority from a certificate of a **<u>Delegation of Authority Order</u>** supported by oath/affirmation issued from congress. Remember ***ignorance is no excuse for the Law***. You must ask for this document or they will proceed without it.

H) Sometimes before a court hearing you will be asked to sign a speedy-trial waiver, this is a waiver asking you to sign away you're Constitutional Rights that will get you off the very ticket that there charging you for. I strongly suggest against signing it if you plan on fighting the charges. You would be literally waiving your rights good bye.

## Trial Questions for Cops

OBJECT to the cops' entire testimony by saying***........."Objection my honor, everything he stated is hearsay and also those are facts not entered into evidence, the only thing that's in my court case file is a citation (***which is just a promise to appear***) and the evidence that I submitted therefore I am unable to properly prepare myself with a fair and just defense" FTR".*** (See what the Judge says) You can also say..... ***for the record my honor if this is a criminal I must also OBJECT because there's no injured party in this manner since this suit/case is considered a crime.*** (See what the Judge says) If they try to dispute that just let the Judge know that Traffic Court is listed under criminal court. If for whatever reason they tell you that it's listed under civil court demand to see a contract with your signature on it along with the other agreeing party. Understand that in most cases the people that I've helped just read off the questions for the cop and get off that way. **If you read questions that pertain to the Judge they would probably feel like you're personally attacking them and they tend to get aggressive. I'm just saying. Essentially it isn't necessary.**

1) What is your true and legal name?
2) Are there any other names, fictitious or not, that you go by?
3) Who is Officer John Doe Badge#1234?
4) Is Officer John Doe Badge#1234 another name that you go by?
5) Is your EMPLOYER the "WHATEVER" POLICE DEPARTMENT (YES or NO)
6) Is that COMPANY registered in the state of California? You can also ask the Judge if they also work for the State. By both having the same employer that goes against court rules.
7) When did your EMPLOYER hire you?
8) What is your official position title?
9) What are your official duties?

10) In performing your official duties, are you required to show identification (YES or NO) If so exactly how many different pieces of identification do you show? Did you know that you are required by law to show 3 forms of ID as proof?
11) In your field experience what is the purpose of identification? Do you volunteer to show proof of proper identification that you are who you say you are?
    Are you the alleged witness in this case? (YES or NO)
12) If your EMPLOYER required you to perform a task against me that was repugnant to the Federal Constitution would you do it? (YES or NO)
13) Does your EMPLOYER require you to take an oath of office (YES or NO)
14) Is that oath to the state and federal Constitution (YES or NO)
15) Did you take that oath (YES or NO)
16) Would you knowingly violate that oath (YES or NO)
17) Do you understand that Ignorance is no excuse for the law? (YES or NO)
18) On the day of the alleged offense were you EMPLOYEED by THE POLICE DEPARTMENT (YES or NO)
19) What time did you start your shift?
20) What time did your shift end?
21) From the time you clocked in until the time you clocked out, Did you or did you NOT engage and or perform duties that were in excess of your delegated authority (YES or NO)
22) Do you know what a Delegation of Authority Order is? (YES or NO)
23) Do you have a Delegation of Authority Order? (YES or NO)
24) Do you know what Treason is Officer John Doe? (YES or NO)
    **Can you please explain to the court the incident that transpired on that day?**
25) On the day of the alleged offense did you use emergency procedures to arrest and detain the defendant (YES or NO)

26) On the day of the alleged offense did you use your emergency police sirens to force the alleged defendant to pullover (YES or NO) When you pulled me over based on your knowledge was I driving?
27) On the day of the alleged offense were you armed with guns, tazer, mase, handcuffs and baton on your person or in your motorized vehicle (YES or NO)
28) On the day of the alleged offense **did you force a bill of attainder/** citation upon the alleged defendant? (YES or NO) When you pulled me over.......was I 'driving' according to law?
29) On the day of the alleged offense did you John Doe and Officer JOHN DOE BADGE#1234 fill out a citation, ticket, summons, Bill of attainder? So what would happen if I don't agree to contract with you by signing my name?
30) Is this you're spelling and hand writing on this citation/bill of attainder?
31) Did you file this complaint? Where did you file it?
32) Would you have knowingly filed this complaint if it was invalid or unlawful? *******
33) Are you alleging that the complaint you filed against me is valid based on your understanding according to the law? *******
34) Does this complaint clearly identify a crime? ********
35) How many elements of a crime are there? *******
36) Does this complaint have all the elements of a valid cause of action? *******
37) How many elements are in the valid cause of action that you allege you filed against me? ********
38) Can you please describe and identify the crime committed in this alleged offense? *******
39) Can you please describe and identify the alleged defendant in this matter?
40) Is the defendant present in court today?
41) Can you point him out?

42) Do you recognize the alleged defendant (me) as a flesh and blood living man/woman standing here before you?
43) Can you please describe and identify the plaintiff in this matter?
44) Is the plaintiff present in court today?
45) Can you point him/her out?
46) Who is the person or individual alleging that I have committed a personal injury or damage to him or her?
47) Is there any evidence of a victim?
48) If you cannot identify the plaintiff, and the plaintiff is not present, and there is NO evidence of a victim, would it be just and fair to say that there is NO plaintiff? ******

## SUPREME COURT CASE RULINGS

"Without standing, there is no actual or justifiable controversy, and courts will not entertain such cases"

***Clifford S. v. Superior Court, 45 Cal. Rptr. 2d 333, 335.***

"Statements of counsel in brief or in argument are not sufficient for summary judgment"

***Trinsey v. Pagliaro, D.C. PA. 1964, 229 F. Supp. 647.***

(Many Judges know this case)

"Standing is perhaps the most important part of the jurisdictional doctrines.....Standing represents a jurisdictional requirement which remains open to review at all of the litigation".....

***'Now, Inc v. Schneider, 510 US 249.***

"A plaintiff must allege personal injury"

***Allen v. Wright, 468 US 737, 751 Supreme Court.***

**KEY NOTE:** The **asterisk** by certain key questions means that one of these questions may trigger the Judge to move to strike the police testimony, throw his testimony out, and rule him as incompetent or inform the Officer not to answer the question(s). It is at this point that you could read these case ruling(s) and politely demand the Judge to dismiss your case. Even if the Judge doesn't rule the cop as incompetent, continue by reading the case laws and politely demand for the dismissal of your case. If for some unlawful reason the Judge still finds you guilty go to the clerk's window and ask for the appeal paperwork and fill it out in a timely fashion.

# *Chapter 10:*

## Trial by Written Declaration

1. (Correctable violations) If the "Yes" box is checked on the front of your ticket, the violation is correctable. Upon correction of the violation, have a law enforcement officer or an authorized inspection/installation station agent sign below. (Veh. Code, § 40616.) Registration and driver license violations may also be certified as corrected at an office of the DMV or by any clerk or deputy clerk of a court. The violation will be dismissed by the court after PROOF OF CORRECTION and payment of a transaction fee are presented to the court by mail or in person by the appearance date. Violations of Vehicle Code section 16028 (automobile liability insurance) will be dismissed only upon (1) your showing or mailing to the court evidence of financial responsibility valid at the time this notice to appear was issued, and (2) your payment of a transaction fee.

| CERTIFICATE OF CORRECTION (MUST BE RETURNED TO COURT) | | | | |
|---|---|---|---|---|
| Section(s) Violated | Signature of Person Certifying Correction | Serial No. | Agency | Date |
| | | | | |
| | | | | |
| | | | | |

2. If you contest the violation (select a or b):

a. (Court trial) Send a certified or registered letter postmarked not later than five days prior to the appearance date or come to the court by the appearance date to request a court trial on a future date when an [illegible] and any witnesses will be present. **You will be required to submit the bail amount.**

b. (Trial by written declaration (traffic infractions)) Send a certified or registered letter postmarked not later than five days prior to the appearance date or come to the court on or before the appearance date to request a trial by written declaration. **Submit the bail amount.** You will be given forms to allow you to write a statement and to submit other evidence without appearing in court. An officer will also submit a statement. The judicial officer will consider the evidence and decide the case.

3. Make check or money order payable to Clerk of the Court. Write your citation number and driver license number on your check or money order. You may pay in person, by mail, or by phone.

4. If "Booking Required" is checked you must appear for booking prior to your court date at 1718 W. 162nd St., Gardena and bring the signed verification to your court appearance. Call 310-217-9500 for more information.

Booking Verification: I declare under penalty of perjury under the laws of the State of California that

__________ was booked on __________ __________ __________
Defendant's name Date Officer Serial No.

5. Additional information is available at: www.lacourt.org

THIS CHAPTER WAS PUT TOGETHER for those who value their time and for those who may be a bit timid in front of Judges and other authority figures. Also for people who truly just cannot afford to take off from their jobs which could add up from 2-3 separate days easily which in many cases is the amount the citation itself. About 5-10% of all ticket holders actually stand up and fight for their rights in traffic court. Hopefully you are fortunate enough you live in one of the following states that permit the trial by written declaration. The following States are ***California, Oregon, Florida, Wyoming, Hawaii, Ohio, Indiana, Louisiana, and Nebraska***. All other states in the U.S. don't currently have this luxury. What I've also noticed is that when people choose to stand up for their rights knowing that they have a very good chance to winning their case those numbers dramatically go through the roof. In other words if 50 people stood up instead of just five folks 40-45 people would more than likely get their tickets dismissed. For those who may be fearful for whatever reason this would be a great opportunity for you to contest your citation because of the fact that you are not going to be verbally going toe to toe with a Judge. A trial by written declaration is having the convenience of handling your court matters without actually going to court. In California held in vehicle code and section 40902 and 40519b which will allow any defendant to challenge a citation in writing, without having to make a private or special appear appearance in court. Notice I didn't say make an appearance in court. This form is called TR-200 and although it may be called something different in other various States. Be sure to check your state for the proper title of paperwork needed. This method saves people lots of time and energy from becoming less motivated when dealing with court which can sometimes take hours and hours and can sometimes take all day long not to mention the headache you might end up with……. literally. You can easily retrieve the paperwork from the website at **www.goodbyetrafficticket.com**. Many companies charge from $175 to upwards of $600+ dollars plus the bail amount per ticket for the exact same process not to mention that it's very simple to do. And I've noticed that within the paperwork that I have its more detailed and specific in nature than the ones I've encountered. Almost everyone is eligible for this process except for people who may have drug, alcohol, or mandatory appearances to show up for court. Remember that this process is only for people whose due date to show up for court hasn't passed and that your ticket doesn't say "mandatory appearance" on it. In the vehicle code it states that you have to pay the bail amount however me personally I've never paid the bail because bail doesn't apply in any way, shape, or form because it's not a legitimate crime. Just refer to the definition of bail and you'll quickly see what I'm talking about. However be sure to use your own discretion so if you feel the need to pay the bail amount and go along with the process please feel free to do so. The bail money goes to a private trust account that they've set up. Me personally I've taken risks to see just exactly what I can and cannot get away with. Remember each experience is different and by not mailing in the bail amount could possibly sabotage the entire process and you may be ask to show up for court and skip the trial by declaration process altogether so have a thorough understanding of the information before you take any risk.

**Important:** By filing a declaration in a trial by written declaration, you are pretty much waiving your rights to remain silent and not incriminate yourself, and the right to a speedy trial. So as far as any written statements within your trial by written declaration I strongly suggest that you don't put anything in writing admitting to any so call wrong doing such as admitting to running a red light or admitting to speeding etc. You're also waiving your right to be heard by a judicial officer of the court, except that you will have a right to a new trial ("Trial De Novo") in court if you disagree with their decision in your trial by written declaration which would mean that they found you guilty.

Please be sure once your paperwork is filled out to make copies (3 copies minimum) of your documents before you have the courts record your documents and always have your mail sent via certified so they can't say that they didn't receive it. In other words make them sign for it. The police officer will also write out a written statement as to what happened in terms of them telling their side of the story. Police officers are paid anywhere from $200-$500 dollars which is easy money to them just to show up in court for a quick appearance which makes them more prone to show up for court however I've learned that they don't get paid anything for filling out the form for your trial by written declaration which I have noticed a significant drop off in terms of them filling out the forms and responding to it in a timely fashion. About 40-50% of officers will not fill it out. Of those that do another 10-20% do not fill it out on time which is good news for you guys. If in the event you are guilty through this process you have about 20-30 days (check with your State to confirm the exact amount of time you have) to get your case heard in traffic court. The process will start over and go straight to trial in deciding your case based on testimonies and evidence presented at court trial, and is not limited by the sentence imposed in the trial by written declaration. Some examples will be in the website listed within this book. In the event that you are presented with a greatly reduced fine or offered to accept a small base fine with no points on your record through this process remember that you can submit to that and take the deal if you choose to. Again it is at your discretion to do so or not. And if you have any further questions on this topic you can always ask a clerk or get a small pamphlet that'll explain it in more detail from any court house. However again it is pretty basic.

For a trial de novo in court, you will have the following rights:

To testify, to present evidence, and to use court orders without cost on your behalf;

To be represented by an attorney employed by you;

To have a public trial;

**AFFIDAVIT OF TRUTH AND FACT**

***Notice Of Non-Acceptance Of Contract (Notice to Appear)***

Comes now, Gregory Dee Garrett Jr., Affiant in good faith and peace to declare his divine prerogative with regard to the herein referenced contract aka *notice to appear* No. G252375. Affiant does hereby give actual notice of his non-acceptance of the contract (notice to appear), and does now rescind his signature on said contract (notice to appear) within the requisite seventy two (72) hour period. Affiant further states that his reason for non-acceptance & rescission is due to the fact that affiant was not allowed to negotiate terms and conditions of said contract (notice to appear), and his signature was given under heavy threat, duress, coercion and under protest, affiant asserts that he was in fear of his life when approached by two (2) men wearing side arms that appeared to be Gardena police officers and began to question affiant and refused to allow him to leave when affiant asked was he free to leave.

These men who assumed a hostile posture when affiant asked what was the nature of their business officers failed to state such, after which he was interrogated at the scene by them and forced to reveal private information affiant fearing for his life was forced to sign the contract (notice to appear) an then was subsequently released from the custody of the men. Affiant is still experiencing significant episodes of anxiety whenever he is in close proximity to men in police cars and wants to put this matter to rest most expeditiously, for all the above reasons affiant is taking the aforementioned action.

Affiant is aware that the issuing agency has the authority to dismiss a notice to appear in the interest of justice pursuant to Penal Code Section 853.6. Subsection (j) paragraph 3, affiant strongly suggests that the issuing agency exercise its discretion and dismiss the herein referenced *notice to appear* in the interest and furtherance of justice, and to insure that affiant avoids any additional adverse psychological and economic effects beyond what affiant has already experienced.

For the record affiant has stricken his signature in red ink on the original contract (notice to appear) so that there is no confusion or ambiguity as to affiant's intentions to void out his signature and evidencing his intention of "non-acceptance of the contract (notice to appear). If any one wishes to contest or object or show verified lawful proof that affiant's actions are invalid and barred by law they must do so within three days of receipt of this affidavit, failure to do so in the required time shall constitute acquiescence of the facts contained in this affidavit and affiant's actions as well, and a waiver of the right to make an objection in the future.

Affiant declares every statement in this affidavit to be true correct and not misleading, and is signed under penalty of perjury of the laws of the state of California.

Dated: February 8, 2017

______________________________
Gregory Dee Garrett Jr, Affiant

Cc: Mark E. Henderson- Mayor Pro Tem
Ed Medrano- Chief of Police
Carolyn B. Kuhl- Presiding Judge LA County Superior Courts
Xavier Becerra- California Attorney general

To remain silent and not testify and not incriminate yourself; to have the witnesses against you testify under oath in court, and to question these witnesses;

Again this is set up according to their rules and regulations that they've put in place.

# *Chapter 11:*

## Lawyers vs. Pro Per

*Isn't it true that every Lawyer that became a Lawyer read certain key books, got an understanding of those books, learned a few laws, became familiar with some rules and a few other things then at the end of their schooling received a law degree? Can't we read those same books (or read a book with the key info within it); become familiar with those same laws and rules of the court? And the only real differences between the two is that one paid an enormous amount of money and received a degree while the other one spent a few dollars and mastered all the same laws with no significance in difference. Now people ask me this particular question all the time as to why should I go into court Pro Per instead of hiring a Lawyer? Now I have a number of reasons but one in particular is that they won't fight as hard as you would in court and on top of that there are certain lines that Lawyers cannot and will not cross.* If you decide to get a Lawyer or an Attorney of the Bar to (British Accredit Registry) Association to (A.B.A.) "re-present" you, realize and understand that you have just surrendered all of your rights to that Officer of the court. From there jurisdiction is assumed, and the officers of the court go straight to the adjudication process as far as fines and fees you're ordered to pay regardless if it gets reduced or not. If it's something a lot more serious like a murder case that's understandable and rightfully so if you are not adept in law I would suggest that you hire an Attorney.

Just remember that Lawyers or Attorneys are officers of the court, and this relationship alone (pretending to be a fair process) constitutes a conflict of interests to you. And if we want to go a little further realize that on an Attorney's bar card it says "at law" however it doesn't say "in law". In law and at law are 2 different things. I can be at your door but not actually inside of your home. Or I can be at the pool but never actually get in the water or even get wet. After understanding this....... do Attorneys have licenses to be lawyers? I'll let you guys figure that one out. Just remember that they 'practice law' (baseball players who practice playing the game are not actually in the game) but when are they going to actually perform or perfect the law? Something else that seems to be a little tricky in law is the word represent. 'Represent' means "to appear" in the character of; to exhibit; and to expose before the eyes. To represent a person is to supply his or her place, to act as his/her substitute; to depict; to mock; to imitate; to act in the character of, etc. These legal phrases, terms, and words are very important, as they pertain to, and affect, the first judicial issue at law which is your and their status.

One who is in their proper person via status (in propia persona pro per) would not allow these judges to refer to them in a 'colored' way or any improper legal term, as anything other than your proper status.

*A lawyer representing you in traffic court could very easily ask for the verified complaint and DEMAND for the dismissal of your case or challenge jurisdiction of the court knowing they don't have it and get your ticket dismissed that way. And again try and remember that their 1st obligation and duty is to the courts and to please the court* ***NOT YOU****. It sounds simple when you think that after you put money into your Lawyers hand that they're going to do their best to get you off right? WRONG.*

# *Chapter 12:*

## Get Over Your Fear

*Face everything and rise or forget everything and run. It's* a distressing emotion aroused by impending danger, evil, pain etc. whether the threat is real or imagined; the feeling or condition of being afraid. ***Synonyms:*** foreboding, apprehension, consternation, dismay, dread, terror, fright, panic, horror, trepidation, qualm. ***Antonyms:*** courage, security, calm, intrepidity. AKA flight or fight. *Well in my opinion it's really 2 fold. Some fear protects us from eminent danger like getting into a fight or being chased by an animal and then there's the stuff that is made up in our heads. The truth of the matter is we are all living with it and dealing with at some point in our lives. Fear is false evidence appearing as real. It's the elusion in many cases. There was a study done on 1,000's of elderly people who were on their death bed in over 80 old folk's homes and were ask the question what is your biggest regret that they had? And they all said in one of their main reasons was that they'd wish that they had being a lot more true to themselves and took more action and not just lived to meet the expectations of others. Wait a minute.......so everybody agreed on the exact same thing? Yes. So with that being said and now knowing after reading this book that infractions are crimes not punishable by imprisonment pursuant to penal code 19.6 here in the State of California (California is a Country) which means that you can't go to jail for a measly traffic ticket, why not stand up for yourself? Why not go into court and literally beat any traffic fine they throw your way? Why not* *learn the law given the fact that it's pretty simple? Why not get involved in something that is a game changer.*

*After millions of people become aware of this particular information the court system will never be the same. So to me it just makes sense to become aware of things to keep lots and lots of dollars in your pocket and not part with it. I can't speak for everyone who read this book but me personally, I like paper money and hate parting with it but that's just me. Leave your mark folks and let this be one of them. This can be one of those stories that you tell your kids/grandkids how you beat your traffic ticket and you can teach it to them as well. I know I am and you should too.*

# *Chapter 13:*

## Know Your Rights

*After watching an arrest on a movie or on a television show if you've ever noticed when the cop puts the handcuffs on whomever they're arresting usually they'll say "you have the right to remain silent, anything you say can and will be used against you in a court of Law". "You have the right to an Attorney, if you cannot afford an Attorney one will be appointed to you…….do you understand your rights that was just read to you"? Think about this…….if we in general know this then why is it that so many people give up their rights when they get approached by an Officer when they ask where are you coming from, or where are you guys headed, or you don't mind if I search your car do you, or do you have any guns or drugs on you? I think that part of the reason is that someone is approaching you with a gun and various weapons on them not to mention their aggressiveness and people in general try not to piss people off with guns. Unless they have reason* ***BEYOND SUSPENSION*** *that you have drugs or weapons in the car (by it being out in the open in your car) or believe that you have committed a crime legally they cannot search your vehicle. But if you give them* ***permission*** *they gain access. This is rule #1 that you should live and die by………don't answer any questions from any Officer unless it's pertaining to your ticket or instructions on a particular violation on your ticket if you choose to because it can and will be used against you in a court of law if it goes there. Just tell them when they start asking a lot of questions that "don't take it personal Officer but I* *don't answer questions". And leave it that. Your lips at that point should be sealed. Rule #2 and this is a big one* ***STOP LETTING COPS SEARCH YOUR CAR WITHOUT A WARRANT****. It kills me when I'm traveling in my personal conveyance and I see 2 people sitting on the curb while cops are going through their personal belongings and breaking a few things in the process. It is a waist your valuable time not to mention the headache. I've seen this time and time again. I've seen soccer moms with their kids, to gang bangers, to college students give up their rights time and time again. People think that because they have nothing to hide or to please the Officers and their wishes or whatever the reason allow these Officers to search their car. STOP IT. News flash.......you have rights. And those rights are protected and secured by the Constitution. Did I mention that they are also God given and that you're born with? And besides they have a tendency to leave your car a mess, they break things by throwing them on the ground (very disrespectful) so why would you just allow someone who you don't know, go through your things, and possibly break your personal belongings? And just in case you didn't think about this but some cops (not all) are criminals who could easily plant drugs in your car and say it's yours and guess what?..........from that point it would be very little that you could do at that point to get from under those charges. It really doesn't make any sense. So please.......I urge you to read the Constitution, the Bill of Rights, your State Constitution, etc. and stop allowing the powers that be take advantage of you simply because you don't know. Well now you know.*

# *Chapter 14:*

## The King Alfred Plan Code Name Rex-84

*Before you start reading this chapter I want you to take a nice deep breath because in this particular chapter will be some very disturbing information that was supposed to been kept top secret by the United States Government and not something that would be somewhat known (most people still don't know about Rex-84) to the public and placed in any book let alone my book. I've actually asked well over five hundred people and only about 2 or 3 were somewhat familiar. When I first read the information it 1st made me almost sick to my stomach then it had me mad as hell. This government that we today call the United States of America(really a business) has been (since the early 40's) planning a massive, violent, and gruesome genocide on the population of so the called African Americans, the so called Hispanics, the Native Americans, and anyone who sympathies with these groups of Indigenous peoples. If you're wondering what "The King Alfred Plan" has to do with a Citation well it is one of the "vehicles" if you will (White Supremacy) that is used to carry out a part of their extermination plot little by little. It's been reported that well over 1,500 murders take place during these quote unquote traffic stops by the hands of murderous police officers yearly. You can actually find some of these murders caught on You Tube, world star, and other various social media channels as well. As we are all well aware (unless you are living under a rock with no TV. or cell phone) that many Officers are using routine Traffic stops to carry out murders all throughout the United States killing thousands of so called blacks and Hispanics (mostly blacks) committing high Treason and getting away with it for the most part with only a small handful of exceptions. This method of killing is being carried out in the name of good old White Supremacy to maintain the present and future existence of white people (actually pink in color) in America and abroad. Although I can't prove my claim of what I'm about to say however it is my belief that we are not too far off of what's to come as far as this King Alfred Plan being put into action. Anyone who may disagree with me on this topic can do the research on the United States Governments track record on doing experiments and or deliberate harm on the population. They just recently poisoned (900 x the legal limit of lead) the water in very high amounts in Flint Michigan (this would fall on the Mayor of that city) that caused many types of ailments (some of which are permanent) on the people in that area. Now the person who will be responsible for issuing the order for "The King Alfred Plan" also known as Rex-84 to take place will be the President of the United States without the approval of Congress, the House of Representatives, or the Senate. Barrack Obama just signed in Martial Law while everyone was focused on Beyoncé's performance at Super Bowl 50 dressed up like the Black Panther from the Panther Party back in the 60's. This brutal genocidal act will be brought into action after something that is called Martial Law. So a heads up that if Martial Law (A National Emergency) is ever called to become active within the entire United States of America knows that it is Rex-84 officially in effect. Actually Martial Law has already been declared it's just that in the near future they will declare it as being active. Here is a small quote piece directly from the information within The King Alfred Plan. "In the event of a wide spread and continuing racial disturbances within the United States King Alfred at the discretion of the President of the United States plan is to be put into action immediately. Participating agencies like National Security Council, Central Intelligence Agency (CIA), Federal Bureau of Investigation (FBI), Department of Justice, Department of Defense, Department of Interior, along with participating State agencies like National Guard Units, State*

*Police, and local agencies like City and County Police. Now in addition to all of these agencies that were just mentioned there were 2 people who decided to come together and further expand on the king Alfred plan which was Oliver North and an ex-President by the name of Ronald Reagan. These were the 2 individuals who amended (upgraded the plan) the King Alfred Plan which then later became Rex-84. I know this because this extensive document was signed by none other than Mr. Reagan himself back in 1984. The 1st or original plan was signed by Linden Johnson which only included only the extermination of black people (property). Mr. Reagan however had to update it and one of the reasons was to include the extermination of the so called Hispanic/Latino population as well. Many of these State Militia groups like the Michigan militia or even the Missouri Militia etc. which are white power military groups that have their training ground out deep in the woods and God knows where else are to be automatically deputize once the President declares Martial Law into action. Many other groups will also be deputized by the Federal Government to assist in rounding up of Black and Hispanic population to be put in prison camps. These prison camps will ultimately be where all will go to die by the hands of the Government carried out and enforced by the military. And allegedly the entire world will implement this same plan to exterminate all if not most of the indigenous people from Africa to South America to Cuba to ensure the survival of the European race. I remember when I was explaining this to one of my friends and they were saying that this "plan" will never succeed because of all of the sympathy that we would be getting from all around the world and I had to explain to them that the Secretary of State developed a policy with Russia and Canada along with many other European Countries. All of these other (European Nations) governments have come together and created what's called a United States European Base to exterminate almost the entire planet. This is why I believe one of the reasons why there sending 200,000 people to Mars to live indefinitely in 2020 is to ensure the survival of certain races on the planet. Now the million dollar question is why? Why are they willing to go to such great and extreme measures to destroy all these people? And why are so called*

*Blacks the "main "target? You would think that the race that taught white people (so called blacks) almost everything they know and also are responsible for the birth of the entire human family wouldn't treat one with such extreme disrespect. One of the reasons I believe is to ensure the survival of the white race because of their recessive nature. The 2nd reason I believe their doing this is because of the deeply rooted hate and fear that they have for the Black race or the 1st Natives to ever walk this planet. The 3rd reason is that these people who are in power are so consumed with power so much so (drunk) that they have become an enemy to our and their very existence. And the 4th reason is that blacks are a stateless people with no Nationality. They're claiming to be something that they are not. This in turn gives them no protection under a Nation. These few families with the most influence and money on the planet have very similar characteristics as to that of cancer. If cancer isn't removed from the body it will ultimately kill its host. And eventually it will die from its own self realizing after it was too late that it only had an existence because it was living off of its victim. Making those that rule parasitic in nature which is why they do what they do. This plan that they have laid out for us is so cold that even within the military they will be separating the so called black and Hispanic soldiers (and other indigenous peoples) and weapons will be immediately stripped away for 'security purposes'. To me it's insane to serve an entity that's planning to destroy for the part all of your family and friends. Their goal is to round up everyone within an 8 hour period to maintain damage control. Even before this horrendous and massive terrorist act is carried out they are tapping phones, watching face book pages, Instagram, Twitter, recording text messages, 24 hour surveillance, etc. I mean you name it and their doing it. All types of cameras onus to the 5th power. In cities and other areas leaders of a wide variety of will be detained 1st and foremost. Watch a movie called "Enemy of the State" featuring Will Smith. That movie will give you a small idea of how their tapping into people's lives without them even knowing about it. Next would be people of progress groups and equality organizations. They even have regions that will be implemented once everything gets going. Ten regions total to be exact. Even the boarders will be on of extreme high alert. On June 27th 1988 George Bush Sr. signed a document order that would turn military bases into prison camps or concentration camps (remember Hitler). The weapons that will be used on the people will have such a tremendous effect on the masses that many will be "micro waved" while standing outside in the open and literally be cooked from the inside out and people will be dropping like flies in large numbers. Whoever insists on not going and cooperating with authorities will be shot dead on site and without any hesitation. This secret military weapon is called V-Mas. It is kept under wraps from the general public. From engaging some of us on the streets via gun battles wide spread to eventually gathering everyone up whose left and ultimately putting us in these incinerators. These incinerators by the way will reach temperatures above 5,000 degrees. This type of fire turns almost completely white. In which these incinerators are reported to not bog down because of its fast burning capacity within almost an instant. I think there will be quite a few of us that will escape the grips of this evil and wicked government plan if it takes place. If for any reason that you think you can escape by leaving with your passport you are sadly mistaken. They will suspend all passports instantly until further notice. So it is of the greatest urgency and importance to have an emergency plan for you and your family for such terrorist acts that may occur from these domestic terrorists. Be sure to have weapons (high powered riffles) to defend your family and home, be sure to stock up on food for a minimum of 90 days or longer, have an emergency back pack in case you cannot gather up all of your tools & equipment etc., have an alternative form of communication other than cell phones, gas masks, life straws that can purify water from almost any source, a compass, have alternative means of travel like a motorbike or a sun power scooter etc., and have more than one spot to call a safe haven. These are just a few things you're going to need to ensure your survival if it ever come to this. I pray that this day never come. Like the saying goes.....it's better to have it and not need it than to need it and not have it.*

# *Chapter 15:*

## Who Is The Plaintiff?

*When it comes to traffic court this is a critical and important question. Most people believe that the cop is the plaintiff. He's truly not. It still puzzles me for people to think this after they have a basic concept or knowledge from seeing court shows on TV where there are always 2 opposing sides. And the cop would be on the side line posing as an alleged witness. And to be quit frank, there not even a real valid witness, they are really observers. They observed you doing something and from there took a report of you doing whatever and gave you a ticket. So what exactly is a plaintiff? A plaintiff is someone that instigates accusations against a defendant in traffic court. In other words the plaintiff is the person who says that you did something to them physically (injury) or monetarily to them and as a result you damaged them some kind of way. It would be the person that would point you out in line up so to speak. Another word to describe the plaintiff would be the victim. A victim is a person who suffers from a destructive or injurious action. Now if you're paying attention the cop isn't the one pointing you out in a lineup right? Of course not because it is the plaintiff who is the one who supposed to be complaining against you and the cop is only the alleged witness. A* **witness and a plaintiff CANNOT BE THE SAME PERSON**. *It violates the rules and laws set up by the structure within the way rules and laws are laid out for the protection of the people. Makes sense right. Now if you don't believe me you can call any random police station in your city/town or ask* *a cop while you're in court what is their position as far as them being the witness or the plaintiff in a traffic case and if there honest with you they will tell you that they are the witness and nothing more. I even had a cop on Hill Street in downtown Los Angeles tell me that he's not even a witness and is just an observer. Now that we've established that in traffic court there isn't a plaintiff and the fact that every single person that I've ever came into contact with said or pointed out the fact to me that there was not a plaintiff in their case. Not one. So in essence it's just you and the Judge. So why are they still pursuing you/us in traffic court? Again and this is my opinion is because this State being that I live in California (other States profit from this as well) is making well over 10 billion dollars annually on traffic tickets and I haven't mentioned parking fines in this manner and how like traffic court is a fraud and is just as guilty of robbing the people in an unlawful and fraudulent manner. So the next time you're at Arraignment for your court case ask the Judge where the plaintiff is. And also ask the Judge if there is no plaintiff in this manner are you acting as the plaintiff today and taking their place, and the Prosecutor, and the Judge? Do you guys see where I'm going with this? It's called a conflict of interests and really a Separation of Powers violation because they can't be all three at the same time and be unbiased at the same time while Judging each case equally. It's impossible people. There pursuing you in court because they have something to gain from this and it is called money..........period. And technically there hasn't been any "money" in circulation since 1933 due to bankruptcy. And it is actually the United States 3rd bankruptcy. So since the plaintiff doesn't exist in traffic court it is my opinion based on law that all citations should be thrown out of the court or never issued from the start because there are never ever 2 opposing sides in the matter. To answer the question in the chapter headline* ***there is no plaintiff****. I hope this is making sense to you all.*

# *Chapter 16:*

## Oath of Office & the Constitutions

### A Standardize Copy of Judges Oath of Office

CALIFORNIA CONSTITUTION

*Section 3: Members of the Legislature, and the all public officers and employees, executives, legislative, and judicial, except such inferior officers and employees as may be by law exempted, shall, before they enter upon the duties of their respective offices, take and subscribe the following Oath or Affirmation:*

*"I, Do solemnly swear (or affirm) that I will support and defend the Constitution of the United States and the Constitution of the State of California against all enemies, foreign and domestic (the ones right next to them); that I will bear true faith and allegiance of the State of California; that I take this obligation freely, without any mental reservation or purpose of evasion; and that I will well and faithfully discharge the duties upon which I am about to enter.*

*"And I do further swear (or affirm) that I do not advocate, nor am I a member of any party or organization, political or otherwise, that now advocates the overthrow of the Government of the United States or of the State of California by force or violence or other unlawful means; that within 5 years immediately preceding the taking of this Oath (or Affirmation) I*

*have not been a member or party or organization, political or otherwise, that advocate the overthrow of the Government of the United States or of the State of California by force or violence or otherwise unlawful means except as follows;*

*(If no affiliations, write in the words "no Exceptions") and that during such time as I hold the office of_______________ (name of office) I will not advocate nor become a member of any party or organization, political or otherwise, that advocates the overthrow of the Government of the United States or of the State of California by force or violence or other unlawful means."*

*And no other Oath, declaration, or test, shall be required as a qualification for any public office or employment. "Public officer and employee" includes every officer and employee of the State, including the University of California, every county, city, city and county, district, and authority, including any instrumentality of any of the foregoing.*

***Things to look up to further your studies***

***A) Articles Of Associations of 1774***
***B) Declaration of Independence of 1776***
***C) Articles of Confederation of 1781***
***D) Treaty of Peace & Friendship of 1787***
***E) US Constitution of 1789***
***F) Bill of Rights of 1791***
***G) Articles of Incorporation of the United States of 1871***
***H) Federal Reserve 1913***
***I) Canon's Law of Romans Civil Law***
***J) HJR 192 June 5th 1933****
***K) Accept For Value***
**L) The Act of 1871**
**M) The Reconstruction Act of 1867**
**N) Declaration on the Rights of Indigenous Peoples 2007**
**O) The Doctrine of Discovery 1724**
**P) Declaration Rights of a Child 1948**

**Q) The Buck Act 1940**
**R) Federal Tax Lean 1966**
**S) Coinage Act of 1792**
**T) Fair Debt Collection Practices Act (FDCPA)**
**U) The Logan Act**
**V) The Motor Carrier Act**
**W) The Alien Sedition Act 1798**
**X) Theft Act 1978**
**Y) Racketeer Influenced & Corrupt Organizations Act 1970**

**Constitution of the State of California 1849**

***Article 1.***

Sec.1. All *men are by nature free & independent*, & have certain inalienable rights, among which are those of enjoying & defending life & liberty, acquiring, possessing, & protecting property: & pursuing & obtaining safety & happiness.

Sec.2. All political power is inherent in the people. ***Government is instituted for the protection, security, & benefit of the people.***

Sec.3. The ***right of trial by jury shall be secure to all,*** & remain inviolate forever.

Sec.5. the privilege of the ***writ*** of habeas corpus shall not be suspended.

Sec.6. Excessive **bail shall not be required**, nor excessive fines imposed, nor shall cruel or unusual punishment be inflicted, nor shall witnesses be unreasonably detained.

Sec.9. every citizen may freely speak, write, & publish his/her sentiments on any/all subjects.

Sec.10. the people shall have the right freely to assemble together, & to consult for the common good, to instruct their representatives, & to petition the legislature for redress.

Sec. 11. **All laws of a general nature shall have a uniform operation**.

Sec.15. No person shall be imprisoned for debt, in any civil action on mesne or final process unless in cases of fraud.

Sec.16. No **bill of attainder (also known as traffic tickets & or citations),** ex post facto law, or law impairing the obligation of contracts, shall ever be passed.

Sec. 19.**The right of the people to be secure in their persons**, houses, papers **and effects, against unreasonable seizures & searches**, shall not be violated; & no warrant shall issue but on probable cause, & supported by oath.

***Article 4***

Sec.27. **A lottery** shall not be authorized by the State, **nor shall the sale of lottery tickets be allowed.**

***Article 6***Sec. 1. The judicial power of this State shall be vested in **one Supreme Court. Special Note: all State Constitutions are pretty much the same with just a few variations.**

***U.S. Constitution Republic* of North America 1786**

**Article 1**

**Sec. 10.**No State shall enter into any Treaty Alliance, or Confederation; grant Letters of Marque and Reprisal; coin money; emit bills of credit;

***make anything but gold & silver coin a tender in payment of debts;*** pass any bill of attainder, ex post facto Law, or Law impairing the obligations of contracts, or grant any Title of Nobility.

**Article 3**

**Sec.1. the judicial Power of the United States shall be vested in one Supreme Court** *& in such inferior Courts as the Congress may from time to time ordain & established (D.O.A.O). The* **Judges**, *both of the Supreme & inferior Courts,* **shall hold their Offices during good Behavior**, *& shall, at stated times, receive for their services a compensation, which shall not be diminished during their continuance in office.*

**Sec. 2.*The trial of all crimes,*** (traffic court is listed under criminal court) *except in cases of impeachment,* ***shall be by jury****; and such trial shall be held in the State where the said crimes shall have been committed.*

**Article 4**

**Sec. 4.*The United States shall guarantee to every State in this Union a Republican Form of Government****, & shall protect each of them against Invasion; & on application of the legislature, or of the Executive (when the Legislature cannot be convened), against domestic Violence.*

**Article 6**

*All Debts contracted & Engagements entered into, before the adoption of this Constitution, shall be as valid against the United States under this Constitution, as under the Confederation. This Constitution and the laws of the United States which shall be made in pursuance thereof; and all Treaties made, or which shall be made, under the authority of the United States, shall be the supreme law of the land; and the* **judges in every State shall be bound there by, anything in the Constitution or Laws of any State to the Contrary NOTWITHSTANDING**. *Which means no Judge can* *stand against anything within the United States Constitution. For a copy of the state and federal constitution you can call 866-272-6272 for assistance.*

**"Submitting ones paperwork"**

**Be sure to submit Motions/Affidavits within 7-10 full business days before your 1st court appearance. Make 3 copies**

1) **Have stamped copies of your writ/Affidavits from the clerk's window with you just in case the Judge/ Commissioner/Referee want to verify it.**
2) **Have both copies of the transcripts (Constitutions) with highlighted areas.**
3) **Have your questions (for Judges& Cop) in front of you for the arraignment process or for your trial.**
4) **If at all possible bring certified copies of the Constitutions (State and Federal) to traffic court.**
5) **Take a blank sheet of paper for possible notes.**
6) **Make sure you bring a hand held recorder or record on your cell phone (some courts do not allow cell phone usage) for all traffic court processes if they allow it.**
7) **Make sure that you become very familiar with the information and notes more than twice before your court date.**
8) **If for whatever reason they use unlawful procedures and still find you guilty, go to the clerk's window and *ask for the appeal paperwork to get it dismissed* that way. Make sure it is filled out before the 20-30 day window or whatever time line they give you. The sooner the better.**

# *Chapter 17:*

## The Appeal Process

*The appeal process is fairly simple at the level of traffic court. You would file your paperwork with the court from which you lost your case usually within a 20-30 day period from the day of the verdict. One usually submits copies of what they already submitted to the court as a defense to be passed on to the Appellate Division. A panel of 4-5 Judges sits on the Appellate Division. As opposed to just one Judge at court trial. The panel reviews the trial all documents to determine rather or not the Judge or jurors made any mistakes. However in traffic court there is no trial by juries. This process takes roughly 30-60 days from the time paperwork is turned in for you to get a response. In most cases the panel will rule in your favor pursuant to the law although I personally think that since all citations are bogus then all appealed cases when fought should be ruled in the favor of the defendant. This appeal paperwork is in each traffic court. They don't promote the fact that you can appeal so be sure to ask for the paperwork right after your trial case is over. It's only a few pages and the form only asks for very basic information along with copies of the paperwork that you originally gave to the court. Keep in mind that an appeal does not postpone the deadline for you to pay your fine or complete any part of your sentence. If you wish to* ***delay the order of judgment*** *against you,* ***you must ask the court at the time of your trial for a "stay"*** *of the judgment. This will delay payment until a decision is reached with your appeal.*

# *Chapter 18:*

## Sample of Paperwork to Help You Win Your Case

*Also writs can be used with this information that will save someone a trip to the court house.*

***Writ in the nature of discovery***

To whom it may concern,
Revenue Agent,
Dear Domestic Terrorist,
Judge/Commissioner,
(These are choices you can choose from)

I Am , A Natural Person, in full life, "In Propia Persona Sui Juris, and not in any way, shape, or form Am I "Pro Se; not an artificial corporate person, Nom de guerre, straw-man, or any other fraudulent, misrepresentation, as scribed in all CAPITAL LETTERS, as dishonorably placed before this court on paper; with corrupt and injurious intent, by the unclean hands of others. I state for the record that no foreign persons, or entities represented by them, have any lawful or credible authority to "Represent" me before this tribunal. I "Present my own Proper Self! I will make a special/private appearance with a copy of the Constitution for the state of California, the United States Constitution, & the Treaty of Peace and Friendship on________ ______________________________ to address the issue at hand.

I demand to see the affidavit of fact/proof stating which law "the red light camera" claim I violated in detail on the date the contract/ticket was issued on citation/Bill of Attainder number________________. I am aware as you are aware that under the Bill of Rights section 10 states that undelegated powers belong to the people and I am the people. All parties responsible for this red light camera violated my right to travel in my land of North West Amexum that I am absolutely indigenous to.

It is an established fact that the United State Federal Government has been dissolved by the Emergency Banking Act March 9th 1933, 48 stat.1, Public 89-719; declared by President Theodore Roosevelt, being bankrupt and insolvent. H.J.R. 192, 73rd Congress m session June 5th 1933-Joint Resolution to Suspend The Gold Standard and Abrogate the Gold Clause dissolved the Sovereign Authority of the United States and the official capacities of all United States Governmental officers, offices, and Departments and further evidence that the United States Federal Government exist today in name only.

I am aware that you are trying to collect monies from me that I have never been issued as stated within the Constitution for the Republic of North America, Article 1 section 10 which states nothing but gold and silver is lawful money as a payment of debt, I consider this an attempt of racketeering and unlawful because I have no lawful money. I am aware that you have taken an oath of office to support, enforce, and preserve the constitution for the United States Republic of North America/Constitution for the State of California that you are bond to by oath/affirmation and I demand that you do your job. I'm also aware that you do not have jurisdiction over me, the matter at hand, and the geographical territory. I demand to see your proof that you are an Article 3 Judge within the Constitutional fold of Government and I demand to see your performance bond.

I also demand to see your Delegation of Authority Order issued to you by Congress of the United States Republic North America. I am aware that there is but one Supreme Court that is superior to all courts and that all inferior court Judges must have a Delegation of Authority Order. If the court room that I will be making a special appearance in is in fact a supreme court, I demand that you produce documents in the instrument of an Affidavit of facts from the injured party proving what Constitutional Law that I have violated. If you cannot produce documents that I have demanded of you, you must dismiss this ticket/contract due to a lack of uniform operation as stated under Article 1 section 11 within the Constitution for the state of California.

Key Note: The Motion below is styled and fashioned for the State of California.

John Doe
In Propria Persona Sui Juris
Executor, Creditor and Beneficiary
C/O 1234 Success Lane
Los Angeles, California Republic (90005)

**SUPERIOR COURT OF CALIFORNIA**
**COUNTY OF LOS ANGELES**

**CENTRAL DISTRICT-METROPOLITAN COURTHOUSE**

| | | |
|---|---|---|
| THE PEOPLE OF THE | ) | COURT CASE #C654321 |
| STATE OF CALIFORNIA, | ) | DRIVER LICENSE #1234567 |
| ET AL | ) | |
| Plaintiff, | ) | |
| | ) | **REQUEST FOR VERIFIED** |
| vs. | ) | **COMPLAINT** |
| | ) | |
| JOHN DOE | ) | *California Vehicle Code 40513 (a)(b)* |
| Defendant | ) | *California Vehicle Code 40518 (a)* |

---

**AFFIDAVIT OF FACT**
**Request for Verified Complaint**

NOW COMES, **John Doe,** corpus delecti, in full life, Living Organic sole, Executor, Creditor, Secured Party and Beneficiary of/for JOHN DOE, never to be classified as civilly dead corporate fiction brought into existence by the presumption of indemsonas. Appearing specially and not generally or voluntarily, but under threat of arrest if I failed to do so, with this **"REQUEST FOR A VALID VERIFIED COMPLAINT,"** stating as follows:

## ARGUMENT

Now comes the Defendant, **John Doe,** the natural person requesting that this and all subsequent pleadings be "liberally construed" pursuant to Haines v. Kerner, 404, U.S. 519, and hereby submitting the above entitled-pleading in the above-captioned matter.

Please take notice that on the day of my SPECIAL APPEARANCE, to be heard in "TRAFFIC COURT" am humbly requesting the filling of a verified complaint the police officer in this manner or the District Attorney's Office pursuant to California Vehicle Code 40513 (a & b) which must be filled at least 15 days prior to this case going to trial pursuant to California Penal Code 1382 (a)(1). The request to file a verified complaint is based upon the fact that I will ***not enter a plea*** at my arraignment, and therefore in accordance pursuant to California (Penal Code section 859.3; Vehicle Code, Vehicle Code section 40513(a), Vehicle Code section 40518) a complaint **MUST BE FILED** that shall be conform to Chapter 2 (commencing with section 948) of title 5 of part 2 of the Penal Code, which shall be deemed to be an original complaint, when the defendant elects not to be prosecuted upon written complaint and I the Defendant will not waive any of my inalienable rights in any way, shape, or form upon the request of the filing of a verified complaint and electing that the prosecution may proceed upon a written notice to appear . I the defendant do not know what the cause of action is in this matter, what the statement of facts are in this matter, who the plaintiff is in this matter, and what remedies is being sought against myself in this matter.

Traffic tickets (or a court summons to appear) do not give any of the above and is thus in violation of due process of Law pursuant the supreme law of the land. (The United States Constitution) California law is absolutely clear on the issue of a verified complaint being filed in order for a defendant to properly and lawfully enter a plea on the record. Filing of notice in lieu of complaint. 1st whenever a written notice to appear has been prepared, delivered, and filed with the courts, a copy of the notice when filed with the magistrate, in lieu of a verified complaint, shall constitute a complaint to which I the defendant may plea "guilty" or nolo contendere. But if the I the Defendant plea other guilty or no contest a verified complaint shall be filed in this matter (commencing with section 948) of title 5 of part 2 of the Penal Code, which be deemed an original complaint, and thereafter proceedings shall be had as provided by law, **except that a defendant may, by an agreement in writing, subscribe by him or her and filed with the courts, waive the filing of a verified complaint and elect that the prosecution may proceed upon a written notice to appear.** (b)Notwithstanding subdivision (a), whenever the written notice to appear has been prepared on a form approved by the Judicial Council, an exact copy of the notice when filed with the Judge/ Magistrate shall constitute a complaint to which I the defendant **MAY** enter a plea and, if the notice to appear is verified, upon which a warrant may be issued. If the notice to appear is not verified, the defendant may, at the time of the arraignment, request that a verified complaint be filed pursuant to California Vehicle Code, section 40513 (a)(b).

California law clearly states that if the Notice to Appear is not verified, the defendant may**, at the time of the arraignment; request that the verified complaint be filed.**

Infraction (s), and under California law, all infractions (like misdemeanors), must be prosecuted by a written complaint. "Misdemeanors and Infractions; prosecution by written complaint. "Except as otherwise provided by law, **ALL INFRACTIONS MUST BE PROSECUTED BY WRITTEN COMPLAINT** under oath subscribed by the complainant. Such complaint may be verified on information and belief. California Penal Code 740. The first pleading on the part of "the people" in the superior court in a felony case is the indictment, information, or the complaint in any case certified to the superior court under section 859 (a). The first pleading on the part of the people in an infraction case is the complaint except as otherwise provided by law. California Penal Code 949. Complainant means "plaintiff" or victim alleging injury, Penal Code 1275, 2nd paragraph; and is a "natural person", Penal Code 959. The law is very clear that if the defendant does not enter a plea, the court is required to file a verified complaint not a notice to appear. An exact and legible duplicate copy of the notice when filed with the Judge/Magistrate shall constitute a complaint to which the defendant **may enter a plea**. California Penal Code 40518 (a). The term **may** when used in law indicates a choice and **not a requirement.** California law clearly states that the written complaint under oath must be subscribed by the complainant or plaintiff. All infractions must be prosecuted by written complaint under oath subscribed or signing by the complaint. California Penal Code 740. Again California law is clear in that the written notice to appear that must be subscribed under oath must also be subscribed by the complainant. A police/peace officer is a witness for the State and cannot serve as the witness for the State while simultaneously as the complainant. A witness is not a complainant. A witness, such as the citing and arresting officer, cannot as a matter of law instigate or initiate prosecution against a suspected natural person. Only the complainant can instigate or initiate prosecution.

Without the filing of a formal, verified complaint, the Court lacks subject matter Jurisdiction over this case. It is black letter law that the filing of a complaint gives the court subject matter jurisdiction to hear a matter brought before it. A court acquires jurisdiction over the subject matter when an action is instituted by the filing of a complaint. 16 California Jurisprudence, 3rd Series, 170 (Courts)

The filing of a complaint is essential to invoke the jurisdiction of the court. **City of San Diego v. Municipal Court,** 102 Cal.App.3d 775

The complaint is the foundation of the jurisdiction of the magistrate. 22 Corpus Juris Secundum 303, pages 456, 457

A trial court's subject matter jurisdiction is triggered by the filing of information alleging commission of a public offense within the appropriate venue. 21 American Jurisprudence, 2nd Series, 480 (Criminal Law)

A formal accusation which charges some offenses known to law is essential for every trial for crime, without which the court acquires no jurisdiction to proceed, even with the consent of the accused. 22 Corpus Juris Secundum 167 (Criminal Law)

Jurisdiction over the subject matter is acquired when an action or proceeding is instituted by the filing of a complaint in a court in the jurisdictional territory competent to hear and determine the particular cause. **People v. Gomper** (1984) 160 Cal.App.3d Supp. 1; **Sharp v. Johnson** (5th Cir. 1997) 107 F.3d 282; **St. James Church v. Superior Court** (1955) 135 Cal.App2d 352; **Silverman v. Greenberg** (1938) 12 Cal.2d 21; **Rupley v. Johnson** (1953) 120 Cal.App.2d 548; **Handy v. Superior Court** (1960) 185 Cal. App.2d 21; **People v. Kepford** (1935) 10 Cal. App.2d 128; **City of San Diego v. Municipal Court** (1980) 102 Cal.App.3d 775; **Burns v. Municipal Court** (1961) 195 Cal.App.2d 777; **People v. Agnew** (1952) 110 Cal.App.2d Supp. 837

A formal accusation is essential for every trial crime, without it the court acquires **NO JURISDICTION TO PROCEED.** 16 Corpus Juris Secundum 230 (Criminal Law) The Court cannot allege that a written notice to appear is a verified complaint simultaneously because California law at Vehicle Code 40513 (a) clearly states ***except that a defendant may waive the filing of a verified complaint and elect that the prosecution may proceed upon a written notice to appear.*** If a written notice to appear (traffic citation) is a verified complaint, how could a defendant possibly waive the verified complaint and elect that the prosecution proceed upon a written notice to appear? It is clearly evident that these two documents are different in nature. If the Court argues and alleges that a written notice to appear (traffic ticket) is a complaint, for purposes of appellate review, if necessary, Defendant gives the Court notice that the written notice to appear does conform to California law at Code of Civil Procedure 422.30, 422.40, and 425.10 and Rules of Court Rule 201 and 501 pertaining to the nature and content of a complaint.

**CONCUSION**

Based on the foregoing which is buttressed against sound legal precedent, the **United States Constitution** which is the ***SUPREME LAW OF THE LAND***, the Court should be based on the overwhelming evidence and dismiss this case in its totality against I the defendant for lack of jurisdiction due to a lack of filing a verified complaint as required by California State law, ***or***, in the alternative, compel the plaintiff to conform to State law and file a verified complaint within 15 days so that I may clearly know what charges are being brought up against me to properly and lawfully defend myself. Thank you in kind

______________

John Doe

Authorized Representative
Executor, Creditor and Beneficiary
Of/for **JOHN DOE**
ALL RIGHTS RESERVED
UCC 1-207 / UCC1-308; UCC 1-103
C/O 1234 Success Lane
Los Angeles, California Republic
(90005)

John Doe
In Propria Persona Sui Juris
Executor, Creditor and Beneficiary
C/O Mailing Address
[City, State Zip] Non-Domestic
(323)000-0000

**SUPERIOR COURT OF CALIFORNIA**
**COUNTY OF LOS ANGELES**
**L.A. COUNTY DISTRICT**
**111 NORTH HILL STREET, Ca. 90003**

| | | |
|---|---|---|
| THE PEOPLE OF THE | ) | CASE#J111222 |
| STATE OF CALIFORNIA, | ) | |
| ET AL | ) | **PEREMPTORY CHALLENGE** |
| Plaintiff, | ) | **AGAINST JUDGE; PREJUDICE** |
| | ) | **AGAINST PARTY** |
| vs. | ) | |
| | ) | |
| JOHN DOE | ) | |
| Defendant | ) | |

---

## AFFIDAVIT OF FACT

NOW COMES, **John Doe**, corpus delecti, in full life, Living Organic sole, Executor, Creditor, Secured Party and Beneficiary of/for **JOHN DOE**, never to be classified as civilly dead corporate fiction brought into existence by the presumption of indemsonas. Appearing specially and not generally or voluntarily, but under threat of arrest if he failed to do so, with this «BRIEF IN SUPPORT OF NOTICE FOR PEREMPTORY CHALLENGE AGAINST PARTY," stating as follows:

## ARGUMENT

I, **John Doe,** corpus delecti, in full life, Living Organic sole, Executor, Creditor, Secured Party and Beneficiary of/for **JOHN DOE**, never to be classified as civilly dead corporate fiction brought into existence by the presumption of indemsonas. State my rights are God given and the Constitution offers a legitimate program to protect those rights which cannot be usurped by government.

"Constitutional provisions for the security of person and property are to be liberally construed, and "it is the duty of courts to be watchful for the constitutional rights of the citizen, and against any stealthy encroachments thereon." **Byars v. U.S., 273 U.S. 28**

Government is the servant of "We the People" and as part of We the People I declare God and the Constitution protect our rights to freedom of religion, freedom of thought, the right to liberty. They are a violation of God given inalienable rights and constitutionally protected rights under the first, the fourth, fifth, sixth, ninth and tenth amendments the legislature had no authority to pass a law that conflicts with the United States Constitution or the California State Constitution. These penal codes are based on Color of Law, lies, fraud and are void from the beginning.

Article 6 paragraph 2 (the Supremacy Clause) of the US Constitution says the Constitution and the laws in pursuance thereof made under the authority of the United States shall be the supreme law of the land. The judges in every state shall be bound hereby. Anything in conflict or repugnancy is null and void of law.

All infringement is forbidden...I claim encroachment, infringement, impingement, usurpation; these codes (Color of Law) are a violation of my rights.

"The Constitution of these United States is the supreme law of the land, any law that is repugnant to the constitution is null and void of law. " ***Marbury vs. Madison, 5 US 137 1803***

The codes requiring a license or attempt to regulate my right to travel puts STATE OF CALIFORNIA in clear violation of the law under **Title 18 US code section 2381** which says that in the presence of two witnesses to the same overt act or in an open court of law if you failed in a timely move to protect and defend the Constitution and honor your oath of office you are subject to the charge of capital felony - treason.

Everyone involved in the persecution of me under these void statues has been a trespasser. My rights secured by the constitution have been violated by these unconstitutional void codes (Color of Law).

When statute codes goes against the Constitution it is null and void of law, it bears no power to enforce, no obligation to obey, purports to settle as if it never existed, unconstitutionality dates from the enactment of such law not from any dates so branded in an open court of law. These codes encroaching upon my right to travel are repugnant to the California State Constitution and the Constitution of these United States.

A state may not impose a charge for the enjoyment of a Natural God given right secured by the Federal and State Constitutions.

No state may convert a secured liberty into a privilege, issue a license and a fee for it and require you to have that otherwise you have committed a crime that is totally unconstitutional.

The codes imposed to regulate the right to travel which is a Natural right is unconstitutional and violates my rights to Life, Liberty, and the pursuit of happiness.

"Personal liberty, or the Right to enjoyment of life and liberty, is one of the fundamental or natural Rights, which has been protected by its inclusion as a guarantee in the various constitutions, which is not derived from, or dependent on, the U.S. Constitution, which may not be submitted to a vote and may not depend on the outcome of an election. It is one of the most sacred and valuable Rights, as sacred as the Right to private property...and is regarded as inalienable." **16 C.J.S., Constitutional Law, Sect.202, p.987**.

"No state shall convert a liberty into a privilege, license it, and attach a fee to it."

**Murdoch vs Penn. 319 US 105 1943**

"If the state converts a liberty into a privilege the citizen can engage in the right with impunity,." **Shuttlesworth vs. Birmingham, 373 US Report 262**

Where rights secured by the constitution are involved, there can be no rule making or legislation which would abrogate them. "**Miranda vs Arizona, 384 US 436**

I have relied upon the United States Constitution and on prior decisions of the Supreme Court, and the exercise of my right to travel freely and unencumbered cannot be construed to violate the law therefore we have a defense against willfulness. There was no evil motive or intent

Therefore the prosecutor cannot prove willfulness and has no case

Defined willfulness as an evil motive or intent to avoid a known duty or tax under the law of moral certainty. **U.S. v. Bishop, 412 US 346**

## Judicial Notice

"Officers of the court have no immunity, when violating a Constitutional right, from liability. For they are deemed to know the law." **Owen v. Independence, 100 S.C.R. 1398, 445 US 622**

"Constitutional provisions for the security of person and property are to be liberally construed, and "it is the duty of courts to be watchful for the constitutional rights of the citizen, and against any stealthy encroachments thereon." **Byars v. U.S., 273 U.S. 28**

The police acting under color of law arrested me without a warrant or probable cause, falsified sworn statements.

This court is obligated to protect the people's rights against encroachment by police acting under color of law. "The court is to protect against any encroachment of constitutionally secured liberty." **Boyd vs. US, 116 US 616**

Failure of the court to protect my right as it is obligated to do, will result in a **U.S.C title 18 section 241,242** and any other violations not mentioned prosecution.

"While acts of a de facto incumbent of an office lawfully created by law and existing are often held to be binding from reasons of public policy, the acts of a person assuming to fill and perform the duties of an office which does not exist de jure can have no validity whatever in law. An unconstitutional act is not law; it confers no rights; it imposes no duties; affords no protection; it creates no office; it is in legal contemplation, as inoperative as though it had never passed." **Norton vs. Shelby County, 118 US 425**

## Other Supporting Law

"If a law has no other purpose than to chill assertions of Constitutional rights by penalizing those who choose to exercise them it is patently unconstitutional."

**Shapiro vs. Thompson 394 US 618** the rights to due process like in the fourth, fifth and sixth amendments.

The right of the people to be secure in their Person. The right of the people to be secure in their persons, houses, papers and effects against unreasonable searches and seizures shall not be violated and no warrant shall issue but upon probable cause supported by oath or affirmation and particularly describing the place to be searched and the person to be seized.

**5th amendment Provisions concerning prosecution**

**Title 5 USC section 556D**

**Title 5 of the US Code, Section 556(d)** states "When jurisdiction is challenged, the burden of proof is on the government." If they deny you due process of the law all jurisdiction ceases automatically. Also **Title 5 section 557 and section 706** apply. They lost jurisdiction when they denied me due process and violated my Constitutional rights.

Rights of the States under Constitution(10th amendment) The powers not delegated to the United States by the Constitution, nor prohibited by it to the States, are reserved to the States respectively, or to the people.

The legislature does not have the power or the authority to take away rights previously secured by the Constitution.

The Constitution is the supreme law of the land and is a contract between We the People and government and is enforceable in favor of We the People in an open court of law and We the People are the beneficiaries. The document should be enforced in favor of me. All power is inherent in the people. My rights have been infringed therefore I demand that all charges be dropped and this fraudulent case against me be dismissed with prejudice.

The Constitution is an iron clad document endorsable in a court of law pursuant to the statutes of fraud. I am demanding my right on the contract to life, liberty and the pursuit of happiness as well as the right to freedom of religion and the right to be let alone. All these rights have been violated by the police acting under color of law, being protected by the prosecutor and the **SUPERIOR COURT OF WHATEVER STATE AND COUNTY TRAFFIC DIVISION all** acting under color of law and lacking jurisdiction. Once due process is violated jurisdiction is lost and can never be regained.

According to the Constitution I am the clearly intended and expressly designated beneficiary of the contract, I want the Constitutional protection in favor of my rights as I am one of The People and the court swore an oath to protect and defend the Constitution. This court has a legal obligation to protect my rights and dismiss this case in the interests of justice. Supported by:

**Section 114 of Am Ju 16TH vol.**
**Sec 117 of Am Jur 16th vol**
**section 155 Am Jur 16th vol**
**Legislative Fiat as unconstitutional**
**section 177 of Am Jur 16th vol**
**declaratory judgments to test constitutionality**
**Federal Declaratory Act**
**section 255 am jur 16th 256 am jur 16th**

The general rule is that an unconstitutional statute whether federal or state though having the form and name of law is in reality no law but is wholly void and ineffective for any purpose since unconstitutionality dates from the time of the enactment and not merely from the date of the decision so branding it. An unconstitutional law in legal contemplation is as inoperative as if it never had been passed. Such a statute leaves the question that it purports to settle just as it would be had the statute not ever been enacted. No repeal of an enactment is necessary since an unconstitutional law is void. The general principles follows that it imposes no duties, confers no rights, creates no office, bestows no power or authority on anyone, affords no protection and justifies no acts performs under it. A contract which rests on an unconstitutional statute creates no obligation to be impaired by subsequent legislation No one is bound to obey an unconstitutional law and no courts are bound to enforce it. Persons convicted and fined under a statute subsequently held unconstitutional may recover the fines paid. A void act cannot be legally inconsistent with a valid one and an unconstitutional law cannot operate to supersede an existing valid law. Indeed insofar as the statute runs counter to the fundamental law of the land it is superseded thereby since an unconstitutional statute cannot repeal or in any way affect an existing one if a repealed statute is unconstitutional the statute which it intends to repeal remains in full force and effect and where a clause repealing a prior law is inserted in the act which act is unconstitutional and void the provision of the repeal of the prior law will usually fall with it and will not be permitted to operate as repealing such prior law. The general principle stated above applies to the Constitutions as well as to the laws of several states insofar as they are repugnant to the Constitution and the laws of the United States. Moreover a construction of a statute which brings in conflict with a constitution will nullify it as effectively as if it had in its expressed terms been enacted in conflict therewith.

**Sec 257 amjur 16th**

Protection of Rights

The actual existence of a statute prior to determination that it is unconstitutional is an inoperative fact and may have consequences which cannot justify being ignored when a statute which has been in effect for some time is declared unconstitutional questions of rights claim to have become vested of status of prior determinations deemed to have finality and enacted upon accordingly of prior determinations and of public policy in light of the nature both of the statute and of its previous application demand examination. It has been said that in all-inclusive statement of the principle of absolute retroactive invalidity cannot be justified. An unconstitutional statute is not necessarily a nullity it may have indeterminate consequences binding upon the people.

**Sec 258 am jur 2nd 16th vol**

On the other hand it is clear Congress cannot by authorization or ratification give the slightest effect to a state law or constitution which is in conflict with the Constitution of the United States.

**<u>Sec 260 Am Jur 16th</u>**

Although it is manifest that an unconstitutional provision in the statute is not cured because included in the same act with valid provisions and that there are no degrees of Constitutionality.

## Conclusion and Relief Sought

**1) Dissolve this debt and Dismiss all charges with prejudice to keep from further violating my rights.**

**2)** I want a hearing on the Constitutionality of the statutes regulation along with my Constitutional right to travel as relating to my fundamental and God given rights to freedom, the right of liberty, freedom of thought, and pursuit of happiness. Even after dismissal of all charges I want the Constitutionality cleared up once and for all. My rights have been violated by these codes, statutes (Color of Law) and I want it to stop. I have a right to be let alone and not harassed by government intrusion.

I, **John Doe,** corpus delecti, in full life, Living Organic sole, Executor, Creditor, Secured Party and Beneficiary of/for **JOHN DOE** and never to be classified as civilly dead corporate fiction brought into existence by the presumption of indemsonas. With allegiance to God and God alone. All Rights Reserved, UNDER THREAT OF SLAVERY, **<u>UCC 1-308, UCC 1-103.</u>**

__________________________________

**John Doe Name**
Authorized Representative
Executor, Creditor and Beneficiary
Of/for **STRAWNAME**
ALL RIGHTS RESERVED
UCC 1-207 / UCC1-308; UCC 1-103
C/O Mailing Address
[City, State Zip]Non-Domestic

# *Chapter 19:*

## Lawful Definitions

**LAWFUL MONEY:** Money which **is** a legal tender in payment of debts: e. g. **gold & silver** coined at the mint. ***Paper bills are only a REPRESENTATION OF MONEY.*** In today's money our paper currency would be considered debtor notes due to the fact that we can no longer walk into a bank and withdraw gold and or silver.

**DRIVER:** ***One employed in conducting (business i.e. making $$$)*** a coach, carriage wagon, or other vehicle, with horses, mule, or other animals, or a bicycle, tricycle, etc. In today's modern time this would be ***A Fed Ex driver, Delivery driver, commercial truck driver, taxi driver, pizza delivery driver, limo driver, uber driver, etc.***

**TRAVELER:** The term is used in a broad sense to designate those who patronize inns. **A Traveler is one who travels in any way**. Distance is not material. A townsman or neighbor may be a traveler, and therefore a guest at an inn, as well as he who comes from a distance or from a foreign country.

**TRAFFIC:** Commerce; trade; dealings in merchandise, bills, money, and the like.

**PLEA**: A suit or action. To be made aware of (**the charges**) actions or suits between private persons. ***The answer which the defendant in an action at LAW makes to the plaintiff's verified complaint, and in which he sets up matter of FACTS as his or her defense***, thus distinguished from a demurrer, which interposes objections on grounds of **LAW.**

**ARRAINGNMENT:** Calling the defendant to the bar of the court, to answer the accusation contained in the indictment ***(or verified complaint).***

**CRIME:** A crime is that which the government notices as ***injurious*** **(bodily harm of some sort)** to the public, and punishes in what is called a **criminal proceeding.** Also **for a crime to be valid there has to be 5 elements** present that actually make up a crime.

**PLANTIFF**: A person who brings an action; ***the party who complains*** *or sues in a personal action* and is so named on the record.

**DEFENDANT**: *The person* ***defending or denying***; the party against whom relief or recovery is sought in an action or suit.

**INDICTED**: Charged in an indictment with a criminal offense.

**INDICTMENT**: An indictment is an accusation ***(verified complaint)*** in writing found and presented by a grand jury, legally convoked and sworn, to the court in which it is impaneled, charging that a person therein named has done some act, or been guilty of some omission, which, by **LAW**, is a public offense, punishable on indictment.

**NAME:** The designation of an individual person, or a ***firm,*** or ***corporation.*** In law a man cannot have more than one **Christian name**. Rex vs. Newman, 1Ld. Raytn.062. As to the history of Christian names and surnames and their use and relative importance in law, see In re Snook, 2 Hilt. (N.Y.) 566.

**TITLE:** The radical meaning of this word appears to be that of a **mark**, style, designation; a distinctive appellation; the uauie by which anything is known. Thus, in the law of persons, a title is an appellation of dignity or distinction, a name denoting the social rank of the person bearing it; as "duke" or "count".

**NATIONALITY:** Belonging to a body politic, Nation or State affording one the protections guarantees security natural and political rights retained by the group. ***Nationality determines the political status of the individual, especially with reference to allegiance***; while domicile determines his/her civil status. Nationality arises either by birth or by Naturalization. According to Sevigny, "Nationality" is also used as opposed to "territoriality", for the purpose of distinguishing the case of a Nation having no National territory, e.g. the Jews. 8 Sav.Syst.346; Westl. Priv. Int. Law, 5.

**HEARSAY:** Broadly, an out of court statement offered to prove the truth of whatever it asserts. **Hearsay evidence is often inadmissible** at trial. However, many exclusions and exceptions exist. Evidence meeting the broad definition may not actually be hearsay under the court's evidence rules. Even hearsay may be admitted if exceptions are met.

**BAIL:** To procure ***the release of a person from legal custody***, by undertaking that he shall appear at the time and place designated and submit himself to the jurisdiction and judgment of the court To set at liberty a person arrested or imprisoned, on security being taken for his appearance on a day and a place certain, which security is called "bail," because the party arrested or imprisoned is delivered into the hands of those who bind themselves for his forthcoming, (that is, become bail for his due appearance when required,) in order that he may be safely protected from prison. Wharton. Stafford v. State, 10 Tex. App. 49.***To make it even more clear bail is to get you out of jail or to prevent you from going to jail. And infractions are crimes not punishable by***

***imprisonment therefore bail does not apply in all traffic cases in any way, shape, or form.***

**COLOR OF LAW:** The **appearance** (***the procedures of traffic court)*** or semblance, without the substance, of **legal right**. McCain v. Des Moines, 174 U. S. 108, 19 Sup. Ct. (H4, 43 L. Ed. 936

**LICENSE** : 1) governmental ***permission to perform a particular act*** (like getting married), conduct a particular business or occupation, operate machinery or vehicle after proving ability to do so safely, or use property for a certain purpose. 2) The certificate that proves one has been granted authority to do something under governmental license. 3) a private grant of right to use real property for a particular purpose, such as putting on a concert***. It simply means that the ability to do something that without it you could never do. In other words their saying that you would be unable to have this ability to "drive" without their permission to do so. And that's called a privilege but what they don't tell you is that you were born with the right to travel and to go to and from where you please.***

**COERCION;** The act of coercing use of force or intimidation to obtain compliance. Force or the power to use force in gaining compliance, as by a government or police force.

**EXTORTION;** The practice of obtaining something, especially money, through force or threats.

**RACKETEER;** A person who commits crimes such as extortion, loan sharking, bribery, and obstruction of justice in furtherance of illegal business activities.

**REPUBLIC:** A commonwealth; **a form of government which derives all its powers directly or indirectly from the general body of citizens**

**(THE PEOPLE)**, and in which the executive power is lodged in officers chosen by and representing the people and holding office for a limited period, or at the pleasure of the people, and in which the legislative power may in trusted to a representative assembly.

**ADMINISTRATIVE:** Pertaining to administration. Particularly having the character of executive or ministerial action. In this sense, administrative functions or acts are distinguished from such as are judicial. People vs. Austin, 20 App. Div. 1, 46 N. Y. Supp 526.

**PRESIDENT:** One placed in authority over others; ***a chief officer***; a presiding or managing officer (magistrate/judge); a governor, ruler, or director. The chairman, moderator, or presiding officer of a legislative or deliberative body, appointed to keep order, manage **the proceedings, and govern the administrative details of THEIR BUSINESS (United States Corporation)**.The chief officer of a corporation, company, board, committee, etc., generally having the main direction and administration of their concerns. Roe vs. Bank of Versailles, 167 Mo. 406, 67 S.W. 303. The chief executive magistrate of a state or nation, particularly under a Democratic (Democracy is a Fraud) form of government; or of a province, colony, or dependency.

**REFEREE:** ***In practice***. A person to whom a cause pending in a court is referred by the court, to take testimony, hears the parties, and report thereon to the court. See Betts vs. Letcher, 1 S. D. 182, 46 N. W. 193; Central Trust Co. us. Wabash, etc, R co. (c. c.) 32 fed. 685

**POLICE:** Police is the function of that branch of the administrative machinery of government which is ***charged with the preservation of public order and tranquility the promotion of the public health, safety, and morals and the prevention, detection, and punishment of crimes***, Police is in general a system of precaution, either for the prevention of crime or of calamities. Its business may be distributed (1) eight district branches: (2)Police for the prevention of offenses; 2 police for the prevention of epidemic diseases; (3)police for prevention of calamities; (4) police of charity; (5) polices of interior communication; (6)police of public amusements; (7) Police of recent inteligade. (8) Police for registration.

**POLICY:** The general principles by which a government is guided in its management of public affairs, or the legislature in its measures. This term as applied to Law, Ordinance, or rule of law, denotes its general purpose of tendency considered as directed to the welfare or prosperity of the State or community.

**SPEEDY TRIAL:** In criminal law. As secured by Constitutional guaranties, a speedy trial means a trial conducted according to fixed rules, regulations, and proceedings of law, free from vexations, capricious, and oppressive delays manufactured by the ministers of justice.

**CONSTITUTION:** (American Law)**:** The written instrument agreed upon by the people of the Union or of a particular state, as the absolute rule of action and decision for all departments and officers of the government in respect to all the points covered by it, which must control until it shall be changed by the authority which established it, and in opposition to which any act or ordinance of any such department or officer is **NULL AND VOID.**

**COURT COMMISSIONER:** A term used variously to designate a lawyer appointed to hear facts report to court…specially appointed officer of the court. ***A person appointed to conduct judicial sales.***

**Infraction:** Infractions are ***crimes not punishable by imprisonment*** pursuant to penal code 19.6 A breach, violation or infringement; as of law, a contract, a right or duty. A violation of statute (**NOT CONSTI-**

**TUTIONAL LAW**) for which the only sentence authorized is a fine and which violation is expressly designated as an infraction.

**JUDGE:** A public officer, appointed **to preside and to administer the law in a court of justice**; the chief member of a court, **and charged with the control of proceedings and the decision of questions of law or discretion**.

**JUDGMENT:** The official and authentic decision of a court of justice upon the respective rights and claims of the parties to an action or suit therein litigated and submitted to its determination. The final determination of the rights of the parties in an action or proceeding. The sentence of the law pronounced by the court upon the matter appearing from the previous proceedings in the suit. It is the conclusion that naturally follows from the premises of **law** and **fact**.

**JURISDICTION:** The power and authority **constitutionally** conferred upon (or **constitutionally** recognized as existing in) a court or judge to pronounce the sentence of the law, upon a state of facts, proved or admitted, referred to the tribunal for decision, and authorized by law to be the subject of investigation or action by that tribunal, and in favor of or against persons (or a res) who present themselves, or who are brought, before the court in some manner sanctioned by law as proper and sufficient.

**JURY:** In practice. A certain number of men, selected according to law, and sworn (juris) to inquire of certain matters of fact, and declare the truth upon evidence to be laid before them. There are subdivisions of juries; the most common jury is a **petit jury.**

**PETIT JURY**: The ordinary jury of twelve men for the trial of a civil or criminal action. So called to distinguish if from the grand jury. A petit jury is a body of twelve men impaneled and sworn in a district court, to try and determine, by a true and unanimous verdict, and question or issue of fact, in any civil or criminal action or proceeding, according to law and the evidence as given them in the court.

**PUBLIC LAW**: That branch or department of law which is concerned with the state in its political or sovereign capacity, including **constitutional** and administrational law.

**SOVEREIGN**: A chief ruler with supreme power.

**AFFIDAVIT**: A ***writ or printed declaration or statement of facts, made voluntarily, and confirmed by the oath or affirmation of the party making it***, taken before an officer having authority to administer such oath.

**OFFICER**: One who is **lawfully** invested with an office. One who is charged by a superior power (particularly by government) with the power and duty of exercising certain functions.

**DE FACTO**: One who is in actual possession of the office or supreme power, but by **usurpation**, or without respect to **lawful title**.

**FRAUD**: consisting of some ***deceitful practice*** **(traffic court)** or willful device, resorted to with intent to deprive another of his right or in some manner to do him an injury.

**DE JURE**: Of right; legitimate; **lawful**, the contrary of **de facto.**

**USURPATION**: The **unlawful** seizure or assumption of sovereign power, or supreme power by force or illegally.

**USURPER**: One who assumes the right of government by force, contrary to and in violation of the **constitution** of that country.

**CIVIL**: in its original sense, this word means pertaining or appropriate to a member of a civitas or free political community; natural or proper to a citizen. Also, relating to the community, or to the policy and government of the citizens and subjects of a state. A civil action is a proceeding in a court of justice in which one party, known as the **plaintiff**, demands against another party, known as the **defendant** the enforcement or protection of a private right, or the prevention or redress of a private wrong.

**CITIZEN**: A member of a free city or jural society, (civitas) possessing all the rights and privileges which can be enjoyed by and person under its constitution and government, and subject to the corresponding duties.

**MEMBER**: One of the persons constituting a partnership, association, corporation, guild, etc. One of the persons constituting a court, or a legislative assembly, etc.

**DURESS:** Unlawful constraint exercised upon a man whereby he/she is ***forced to do some act against his will.***

**ASSAULT**: An unlawful attempt or offer, on the part of one man, with force or violence, to inflict a bodily hurt upon another.

**Corpus Juris Secundum:** ***Corpus Juris Secundum*** (***CJS***) is an encyclopedia of United States law at the federal and state levels. It is arranged into over 430 topics, which in turn are arranged into subheadings. As of 2010[update], *CJS* consisted of 164 bound volumes, 5 index volumes and 11 table of cases volumes.[1]

*CJS* is named after the 6th century *Corpus Juris Civilis* of the Byzantine Emperor Justinian I, the first codification of Roman law and civil law. The name ***Corpus Juris literally means "body of the law"***; *Secundum* denotes the second edition of the encyclopedia, which was originally issued as *Corpus Juris* by the American Law Book Company (from 1914 to 1937).[1]*CJS* is published by West in print form and on Westlaw. The print edition is updated annually with pocket supplements and revised editions of bound volumes. Before Thomson's acquisition of West, CJS competed against the *American Jurisprudence* legal encyclopedia.[1]

While legal encyclopedias like *CJS* were at one time heavily used by the courts, the growth of statutory and regulatory governance has had the effect of eroding this reliance. As such, rather than being used as sources of authoritative statements of law, legal encyclopedias will be more often used as tools for finding relevant case law

**THREAT**: A declaration of one's purpose or ***intention to work injury or harm to the person, property, or rights of another.***

**BELIEF**: A conviction of the truth of a proposition, ***existing subjectively in the mind***, induced by argument, persuasion, or proof addressed to the judgment.

**DEMURRER**: The formal mode of disputing the sufficiency in law of the pleading of the other side.

**PERJURY**: ***The violation of breaching an oath*** that has been entered on the record.

**OATH**: An external pledge made in verification of statements made or to be made or with an invocation to a supreme being to witness the words of the party and to visit him with punishment if they be false.

**CORPORATION:** An ***artificial person*** or entity created ***by or under the authority of the laws of a state or nation***, composed, in some rare instances, of a single person and his successors, being the incumbents of a particular oltice, but ordinarily consisting of an association of numerous individuals, who subsist as a body politic under a special denomination, which is regarded In law as having a personality and existence distinct from that of its several members, and which is, by the same authority, vested with the capacity of continuous succession, irrespective of changes in its membership, either in perpetuity or for a limited term of years, and of acting as a unit or single individual in matters relating to the common purpose of the association, within the scope of the powers and authorities conferred upon such bodies by law. See Case of Sutton's Hospital, 10 Coke. 32; Dartmouth College v. Woodward, 4 Wheat. 518, 636, 657.4 L. Ed. 629;

**ADJUDICATION:** The giving or pronouncing a judgment or decree in a cause; also the judgment given. The term is principally used in bankruptcy proceedings, the adjudication being the order which declares the debtor to be a bankrupt. In French law. A sale made at public auction and upon competition. Adjudications are voluntary, judicial, or administrative. Duverger. In Scotch law. A species of diligence, or process for transferring the estate of a debtor to a creditor, carried 011 as an ordinary action before the Court of Session. A species of judicial sale, redeemable by the debtor. A decretal' the lords of session, adjudging and appropriating a person's lands, hereditaments, or any heritable right to belong to his creditor, who is called the "adjudge," for payment or performance. Bell; Ersk.Inst, c. 2.tit. 12,

**VENUE:** In pleading and practice. A neighborhood; the neighborhood, place, or county in which an injury is declared to have been douse, or fact declared to have happened. 3 Bl. Comm. 204. Venue also denotes the county in which an action or prosecution is brought for trial, and which is to furnish the panel of jurors. To "change the venue" is to transfer the cause for trial to another county or district. In the common-law practice, the venue is that part of the declaration in an action which designates the county in which the action is to be tried.

**ARTIFICIAL PERSON:** A ***nonhuman*** entity that is created by law and is legally different owning its own rights and duties. AKA juristic person and legal person. Refer to body corporate

**SUI JURIS:** Lat Of his own right; possessing full social and civil rights; not under any legal disability, or the power of another, or guardianship. Having capacity to manage one's own affairs; not under legal disability to act for one's self. Story, Ag

**ATTORNEY:** In the most general sense this term denotes an agent or substitute, or one who is appointed and authorized to act in the place or stead of another. In re Ricker, 60 N. H. 207, 29 Atl. 559, 24 L. R. A. 740; Eichelberger v. Sifford, 27 Md. 320. It is "an ancient English word, and signified one that is set in the turn, stead, or place of another; and of these some be private * * * and some be public, as attorneys at law." Co. Litt.516, 128a; Britt 2856. One who is appointed by another to do something in his absence, and who has authority to act in the place and turn of him by whom he is delegated. When used with reference to the proceedings of courts, or the transaction of business in the courts, the term always means "attorney at law," q. v. And see People v. May, 3 Mich. 605; Kelly v. Herb, 147 Pa. 503, 23 Atl. 889; Clark v. Morse, 16 La. 576

**IN PROPRIA PERSONA***: In* ***one's own proper person***. In whatever thing one offends, in that is he rightfully to be punished. Co. Litt.2336; Wing. Max. 204, max. 58. The punishment shall have relation to the nature of the offense

**CRIMINAL COURT:** the name of the court where criminal cases are tried and not civil case

**CONTRACT LAW:** Group of laws that control oral or scripted agreements related to trade of commodities and services, properties and money. It also contains topics related to qualities of contractual duties, restriction of activities, liberty of contract, privacy of contract, conclusion of contract, and also contains agency relationships, business document, and deals of employment

**CITATION:** In. A writ issued out of a court of competent jurisdiction, **commanding** a person therein named ***to appear on a day*** (this is not a verified complaint)named and do something therein mentioned, or show cause why he should not. Proc. Prac. Also known to be called a Bill of Attainder which forbidden by law. The act by which a person is so summoned or cited. It is used in this sense, in American law, in the practice upon writs of error from the States supreme, and in the proceedings of courts of probate in many of the states. This is also the name of the process used in the English ecclesiastical, probate, and divorce courts to call the defendant or respondent before them. 3 Bl. Comm. 100; 3 Steph. Comm. 720.In Scotch practice. The calling of a party to an action done by an officer of the court under a proper warrant. The service of a writ or bill of summons. Paters. Comp

**DENATIONALIZATION:1.** to deprive of national rights or characteristics. **2.** To transfer (an industry, for example) from governmental to private ownership

**DEMOCRACY:** That form of government in which the sovereign power resides in and is exercised by the whole body of free citizens; as distinguished from a monarchy, aristocracy, or oligarchy. According to the theory of a pure democracy, every citizen should participate directly in the business of governing, and the legislative assembly should comprise the whole people. But the ultimate lodgment of the sovereignty being the distinguishing feature, the introduction of the representative system does not remove a government from this type. However, a government of the latter kind is sometimes specifically described as a "representative democracy." **Key note, Democracy is not found in the United States Constitution or the meaning or its implementation of its workings.**

**<u>DUE PROCESS OF LAW</u>:** Law in its regular course of administration through courts of justice. 3 Story, Const.264, 661. "***Due process of law in each particular case means such an exercise of the powers of the government as the settled maxims of law permit and sanction, and under such safeguards for the protection of individual rights*** as those maxims prescribe for the class of cases to which the one in mention belongs." ***In other words it is a process that is due to you through court lawful procedures and practices.*** Cooley, Const. Lira. 441. Whatever difficulty may be experienced in giving to those terms a definition which will embrace every permissible exertion of power affecting private rights, and exclude such as is forbidden, there can be no doubt of their meaning when applied to judicial proceedings. They then mean a course of legal proceedings according to those rules and principles which have been established in our systems of jurisprudence for the enforcement and protection of private rights. To give such proceedings any validity, there must be a tribunal competent by its constitution

**<u>DUE PROCESS</u>:** The essential elements of Due Process of Law are notice and opportunity to defend. By ***Due Process is meant a law which hears before it condemns*** which proceeds upon inquiry, and ***renders judgment only after trial.*** **<u>Also known as the process that is due to you</u>**.

**<u>DEFAULT</u>:** The failure to fulfill a duty, observe a promise, discharge an obligation, or perform an agreement. State v. Moores, 52 Neb. 770, 73 N. W. 299; Osborn v. Rogers, 49 Hun, 245, 1 N. Y. Supp. 623; Mason v. Aldrich, 36 Minn. 283, 30N. W. SS4.practice. Omission; neglect or failure. When a defendant in an action at law omits to plead within the time allowed him for that purpose, or fails to appear on the trial, he is said to make default, and the judgment entered in the former case is technically called a "judgment by default" 3 Bl.

**<u>PRO PER</u>:** short for "propia persona", which is Latin for "for oneself" usually applied to a person who represents themselves

**STATUS:** An Individual's **status** is a legal position held in regards to the rest of the community and not by an act of law or by the consensual acts of the parties, and it is *in rem*, i.e. these conditions must be recognized by the world. It is the qualities of universality and permanence that distinguish status from consensual relationships such as employment and agency. Hence, a person's status and its attributes are set by the law of the domicile if born in a law state, or by the law of nationality if born in a civil law state and this status and its attendant capacities should be recognized wherever the person may later travel.

**CONSENT: a voluntary agreement to another's proposition**. 2) v. to voluntarily agree to an act or proposal of another, which may range from contracts to sexual relations

**SHERIFF:** n. the ***top law enforcement officer*** for a county, ***NORMALLY ELECTED***, responsible for police protection outside of incorporated cities, management of the county jail, and providing bailiffs for protection of the courts. A sheriff also handles such civil activities as serving summons, subpoenas and writs, conducting judgment sales, and fulfilling various functions ordered by the courts. The office was brought to the United States from England and is unknown in most nations which use federal and state police. Canada, for example, has the highly-professional Royal Canadian Mounted Police (and its Quebec equivalent) for most police work outside cities. The position of sheriff has been criticized as lacking training standards, being overly political, not being coordinated with other jurisdictions, and being hampered by its lack of authority beyond the county line except when in "hot pursuit" of a suspect who crosses the county line. The sheriff's uniformed police are called "deputy sheriffs," with the number two person often entitled "under sheriff." (See: bailiff, sheriff's sale

**TREASON:** ***The offense of attempting to overthrow the government of the state to which the offender owes allegiance; or of betraying the***

***state*** into the hands of a foreign power. Webster. In England, treason is an offense particularly directed against the person of the sovereign, and consists (1) in compassing or imagining the death of the king or queen, or their eldest son and heir; (2) in violating the king's companion, or the king's eldest daughter unmarried, or the wife of the king's eldest son and heir; (3) in levying war against the king in his realm; (4) in adhering to the king's enemies in his realm, giving to them aid and comfort in the realm or elsewhere, and (5) slaying the chancellor, treasurer, or the king's justices of the out bench or the other, justices in eyrie, or justices of assize, and all other justices assigned to hear and determine, being in their places doing their offices. 4 Steph. Comm. 1S5-103; 4 Bl. Comm. 76-84. "Treason against the United States shall consist only in levying war against them, or in adhering to their enemies, giving them aid and comfort." U. S. Constitution, art 3,

**Waiver:**1. General. (1) Implied voluntary relinquishment, ***abandoning a legal or lawful advantage***, need, claim, or right. (2) Document effecting the abandoning or relinquishing. **This means to basically give up your rights.**

**Bias:** Inclination; bent; prepossession: ***a preconceived opinion; a predisposition to decide a cause or an issue in a certain way,*** which does not leave the mind perfectly open to conviction. Maddox v. State, 32 Ga. 5S7, 79 Am. Dec. 307; Pierson v. State, 18 Tex. App. 55S; Hinkle v. State, 94 Ga. 595, 21 S. E. 601. This term is not synonymous with "prejudice." By the use of this word in a statute declaring disqualification of jurors, the legislature intended to describe another and somewhat different ground of disqualification. A man cannot be prejudiced against another without being biased against him; but he may be biased without being prejudiced. Bias is "a particular influential power, which sways the judgment; the inclination of the mind towards a particular object." It is not to be supposed that the legislature expected to secure in the juror a state of mind absolutely free from all inclination to one side or the other.

**Conflict of Interests:** 1. a situation that can undermine a person due to self-interest and public interest. 2. a situation when parties discharge responsibility to a third party.

**Separation of Powers:** a constitutional principal limiting powers vested in an institution or person. Governmental authority is divided into ***3 branches: Legislative, executive and judiciary.***

**Lawsuit:** A vernacular term for a suit, action, or cause instituted or depending ***between two private persons (in traffic court it's only YOU)*** in the courts of law

**Magistrate:** A public officer belonging to the civil organization of the state, and invested with powers and functions which may be either judicial, legislative, or executive. But the term is commonly used in a narrower sense, designating, in England, a person entrusted with the commission of the peace, and, in America, one of the class of inferior judicial officers, such as justices of the peace and police justices. A magistrate is an officer having power to issue a warrant for the arrest of a person charged with a public offense. Pen. Code Cal. (Magician aka magic or tricks)

**DETAIN:** To retain as the possession of personality. ***TO ARREST***, to check, to delay, to hinder, to hold, or **keep in custody**, to retard, to restrain from proceeding, to stay, to stop. People v. Smith, 17 Cal.App.2nd 468, 62 P.2d 436, 438;

**VOID AB INITIO:** A contract ***is null and void from the beginning if it seriously offends law*** or public policy in contrast to a contract which is merely voidable at the election of the parties to the contract.

**ACQUIESCENCE:** In law, acquiescence occurs ***when a person knowingly stands by without raising ANY OBJECTION to the infringement or abuse of their rights.***

**MOTION:** In United, a **motion** is a procedural device to bring a limited, contested issue before a court for decision. It is a request to the judge (or judges) to make a decision about the case.[1] Motions may be made at any point in administrative, criminal or civil proceedings, although that right is regulated by court rules which vary from place to place. The party requesting the motion may be called the *movant*, or may simply be the *moving party*. The party opposing the motion is the *nonmoving* or *nonmoving party*.

**LIBERTY:** **Liberty** is the quality individuals have to control their own actions. Different concepts of liberty articulate the relationship of individuals to society in different ways. Some concepts relate to life under a *social contract*, existence in an imagined *state of nature*, and therefore define the active exercise of freedom and rights essential to liberty in corresponding ways. Understanding liberty involves how we imagine, and structure, individual's roles and responsibilities in society in terms of free will and determinism, which involves the larger domain of metaphysics.

Classical liberal concepts of liberty typically consist of freedoms of individuals from outside compulsion or coercion, also known as negative liberty. This conception of liberty, which coincides with the libertarian point-of-view, suggests that people should, must, and ought to behave according to their own free will, and take responsibility for their actions. In contrast, social liberal conceptions of liberty (positive liberty) place an emphasis upon social structure and agency and is therefore directed toward ensuring egalitarianism. In feudal societies, a "liberty" was an area of allodial land where the rights of the ruler or monarch were waived.

**BANK:** A **bank** is a financial institution and a financial intermediary that accepts deposits and channels those deposits into lending activities, either directly by loaning or indirectly through capital markets. A bank links together customers that have capital deficits and customers with capital surpluses. A bench or seat; the bench of justice; ***the bench or tribunal occupied by the Judges; the seat of judgment; a court.***

# *Chapter 20:*

## What is Color of Law

Color of law is an appearance of legal power to act but which may operate in violation of the law. It's like a hybrid plant verses the natural plant or you run into someone who looks exactly like someone you know but it's not them. It's trying to mimic the real thing to fool or deceive you through unlawful processes. Another example of this would be someone posing as a police officer acting under "colorable authority" to detain/arrest an individual, if such an arrest is made without probable cause and or warrant the arrest just may be in violation of the law. Another example of this would be anyone who is or have gone or is going through the process of traffic court. If we all have the right to a speedy trial which is 30 days or less and the clerk gives you a court date 8 months from the day it would be more than fair to say that they are using "color of law" to process your court date because they are not within the legal limit of 30 days which is the time frame or limit their supposed to give someone hence speedy trial. Or let's say that you're in court speaking with the judge during arraignment and your demanding that they prove jurisdiction for the record before the case moves forward and they force your hand so to speak by telling you that your options are to plead guilty, not guilty, or no contest (which is just a fancy way of saying guilty) and that you are not allowed to speak on any other matter except on the issue of making a plea. Now this may seem legit giving the fact that people usually make pleas during arraignment in court however this would be considered “colorable procedures” because they are supposed to allow you the defendant to make a plea only AFTER you are made aware of the charges from the plaintiff in the matter who would be physically present on the day of arraignment. So keep in mind that anytime during any proceedings when it comes to traffic court if they are not abiding by the law within their legal limits they are in fact colored. So just know that from our stand point we are operating under color of law from the time that you are being pulled over up to the final point of the judge rendering a verdict of guilty or not guilty. Some of these colorable procedures would be called “colorable codes”, “colored detainment and arrest”, “colorable courts”, “colorable law enforcement”, “colorable judges” and the list goes on and on.

# *Conclusion*

*It is my opinion that there are many cops who are on the police force who do a good job (we need more cops to come forward to fight for justice) in terms of keeping the public safe. In terms of the way police officers are presently being trained we need a 360degree change as how they are being trained. One of those changes would consist of knowing the Constitution through and through. However there are many more police officers who are not civilized and or human in my opinion. Let me define what a human is. To be human to me is to be civilized. You have a set of principles and guidelines that would keep you and your nature and behavior in check and to be a peaceful person. Being able to use discretion so that you don't have the desire to want to go out and harm or kill someone for no real apparent reason nor do you yourself want to be harmed or killed. For the most part because of so many bad apples and other Officers not standing up (you guys are supposed to arrest ANYONE who commits a murder(s) to defend the Constitution against all enemies foreign and DOMESTIC) and arresting these domestic terrorist and because of this the entire police establishment itself right here in North America is a parasitic entity created by bond holders so that they can service the manipulation of fear, and resources from the masses of the people. And what most people don't understand is that crime is actually necessary to operate this shadow fictitious government because it literally thrives on it. No crime, no District Attorney's office, no District Attorney's office no city, no township, etc. So when you hear a Politician telling the public that they want to lower crime rates in your city and State they are flat out lying to you.....allegedly. I could have easily written a 1,500 page book on this subject matter explaining many other concepts and situations however we the people need this vital information urgently with real solutions and understanding.*

*And this is why I got straight to the point in this book. I hope you all enjoyed it. I had fun writing it. It was very challenging and definitely well worth it. Will there be a part 2 to this book? I guess you'll just have to wait and see. Good luck and good study to all those who enforce the Constitution. For more information go to* **www.goodbyetrafficticket.com**

## Traffic Court Quiz (True or False)

*A Judges main objective in Traffic Court is to ultimately seek justice for offenses carried out by the people. True___ False___*

*A real police officer has the right to pull you over if you run a red light while almost hitting a car in the process. True___ False___*

*When a police officer pulls you over you are at that very moment under arrest even if you didn't do anything wrong. True___ False___*

*The plaintiff who is not present in traffic court would be the "People of the State" of where ever you live True___ False___*

*If you were found guilty in traffic court on 4 charges you can get those charges dismissed through the appeal process. True___ False___*

## Traffic Court Quiz (Multiple Choices)

***How many forms of identification is law enforcement supposed to show the people while on duty?***

*A 1___*

*B 2___*

*C 3___*

*D 4___*

*E none___*

***Name the 3 sides or angles of a courtroom tribunal.***

*A judge-witness-observer___*

*B defendant-plaintiff-judge___*

*C defendant-Prosecutor-witness___*

*D judge-Prosecutor-defendant___*

***About what year was Traffic Court established in the Constitutional fold of government?***

*A after 1933___*

*B before 1913___*

*C when commercial rules were set up for driving___*

*D never___*

***In court who does the Judge truly work for?***

*A the people___*

*B the State who pays them___*

*C the County___*

*D the United States Corporation ___*

***In traffic court if the red light camera catches you running a red light can you still prove that you're innocent?***

*A yes___*

*B no___*

*C sometimes___*

*D only if it doesn't show your face on camera___*

*Answers to the Quiz (True or False)*
*False*
*False*
*True*
*True*
*True*

*Answers to the Quiz (Multiple Choices)*
*C*
*B*
*D*
*A*
*A*

Made in the USA
Columbia, SC
26 April 2019